DOLOMITES TRAVEL GUIDE 2023

Discover Adventure, Culture, and Breathtaking Landscapes in Italy's Enchanting Dolomites Region

DAISY MORRIS

Copyright © 2023 by Daisy Morris

All rights reserved. No part of this publication may be reproduced, distributed, or transmitted in any form or by any means, including photocopying, recording, or other electronic or mechanical methods, without the prior written permission of the publisher.

TABLE OF CONTENTS

INTRODUCTION 7
About Dolomites 8
The Dolomites' history 9

CHAPTER 1 13
PLANNING YOUR TRIP TO THE DOLOMITES 13
When to Go 13
Where to Stay 15
How to Get Around 16
What to See and Do 18
Choosing the Right Accommodations in Dolomites 20
Packing List for the Dolomites 26
Dolomites Visa and Entry Requirements 30
The Dolomites' money and language 36
Budget advice for the Dolomites 38
Dolomites money-saving advice: 42

CHAPTER 2 49
TOP ATTRACTIONS IN THE DOLOMITES 49
Go hiking 49
Visit the lovely lakes 49

Drive the mountain passes 49

Visit Val di Funes 50

Ride the Freccia nel Cielo Cable Car to Cima Tofana. 50

Ride the Cable Car to Seceda 50

Ski or snowboard 51

CHAPTER 3 53

DOLOMITES BEST RESTAURANTS AND CAFÉS 53

International cuisine in the Dolomites 58

Cafés And Bakeries In The Dolomites 59

CHAPTER 4 61

THE DOLOMITES' NIGHTLIFE AND ENTERTAINMENT 61

Dolomites bars and nightclubs: 62

Places To Hear Live Music In The Dolomites 64

Dolomite Theatres And Performances 66

CHAPTER 5 69

IN THE DOLOMITES, SHOPPING 69

Gifts and souvenirs in the Dolomites: 71

The Dolomites' Attire And Accessories 74

The Dolomites' Food and Drink 75

CHAPTER 6 81

DOLOMITE OUTDOOR RECREATION 81

The Dolomites' Parks and Gardens 84

Dolomite Walking and Cycling Tours 89

The Dolomites during the winter 93

CHAPTER 7 97

LOCATIONS NEAR THE DOLOMITES 97

Bolzano 97

Garda Lake 98

Venice 98

Verona 99

CHAPTER 8 101

ITINERARY FOR 7 DAYS IN THE DOLOMITES 101

Day 1 Bolzano and Lake Carezza 102

Day 2 Sella Ronda and Cortina d'Ampezzo 103

Day 3: Lake Misurina and the Tre Cime di Lavaredo 104

Day 4: Val Gardena and Alpe di Siusi 105

Day 5: Funes Valley and Lake Braies 107

Day 6: Passo Giau and Marmolada 108

7th day: Departure 110

CHAPTER 9 111

PRACTICAL INFORMATION AND TIPS FOR DOLOMITES 111

Etiquette and Customs in Dolomites 111

Knowing Some Basic Dolomite Phrases 115

Health and safety tips in the Dolomites 123

A List Of Dolomites Emergency Contacts 128

Access to the Internet and communication in the Dolomites 130

Useful apps and websites in the Dolomites: 133

Conclusion 136

INTRODUCTION

I had always dreamed of visiting the Dolomites, the majestic mountain range in northern Italy. So when I finally got to go there for a week. I packed my bags, grabbed my camera, and boarded the plane.

The first thing that struck me when I arrived was the beauty of the landscape. The Dolomites are part of the Alps but have unique character and charm. They are composed of limestone and dolomite rock, which gives them a pale pink hue in the sunlight. They are also dotted with green valleys, blue lakes, and quaint villages.

I decided to stay in a cozy chalet in the town of Cortina d'Ampezzo, which is known as the "Queen of the Dolomites." It was a perfect base for exploring the surrounding area. Every day, I would take a different hiking trail, marveling at the views and breathing in the fresh air.

I saw famous peaks like the Tre Cime di Lavaredo, the Marmolada, and the Tofane. I also visited historical sites, such as the First World War trenches and memorials. One of the highlights of my trip was taking a cable car to the top of Lagazuoi, a 2,778-meter-high mountain.

From there, I had a panoramic view of the entire Dolomite range. It was breathtaking. I felt like I was on top of the world. I shot many pictures in an effort to capture the splendor and majesty of the sight.

Another memorable experience was visiting a traditional restaurant and tasting local cuisine. The Dolomites have a rich and diverse culinary heritage, influenced by Italian, Austrian, and Ladin cultures.

I enjoyed dishes such as canederli (bread dumplings), speck (smoked ham), polenta (cornmeal porridge), and strudel (pastry filled with apples or cherries). I also drank some local wines, such as Lagrein and Gewürztraminer.

My first vacation trip to the Dolomites was an unforgettable adventure. I felt like I had entered a fairy tale world of magic and wonder. I learned a lot about the history and culture of the region, and I made some new friends along the way. I can't wait to go back and discover more of its secrets.

About Dolomites

The Dolomites mountain region in northeastern Italy is well known for its craggy peaks, picturesque valleys, and rich cultural diversity. They stretch from the River Adige in the west to the Piave Valley in the east and are a component of the Southern Limestone Alps.

The Dolomites comprise seven Italian provinces and three regions, totaling 15,942 square kilometers. They are a well-liked location for cycling, climbing, hiking, and skiing and were named a UNESCO World Heritage Site in 2009.

The Dolomites' history

A fascinating and historic history may be found in the Dolomites, a mountain region in northeastern Italy. The French mineralogist Déodat Gratet de Dolomieu originally described the dolomite rock as a carbonate rock in the 18th century. Almost 250 million years ago, the Triassic Period was formed when the Dolomites were created, a significantly older period.

Triassic Era: A Tropical Sea

A warm, shallow, quiet tropical sea that was a portion of the Tethys primordial ocean covered the region that is now the Dolomites during the Triassic Period. Diverse marine life flourished in this sea, including corals, algae, mollusks, crinoids, and ammonites. These animals created Massive reef structures and accumulated over millions of years on the ocean floor.

Most reefs comprised calcium carbonate, which later transformed into limestone and dolomite rock.

Intense volcanic activity also occurred throughout the Triassic Period, which produced volcanic rocks, including porphyry and basalt. The Latemar and Rosengarten groups, two Dolomite regions, include some of these rocks. After the Triassic Period, some 200 million years ago, volcanic eruptions also affected the extinction of numerous marine species.

The rise of the Alps during the Jurassic Period

Significant tectonic movements throughout the Jurassic Period changed Earth's surface from 200 to 145 million years ago. As Pangaea, the supercontinent, broke into smaller continents, the Tethys Ocean began to close. The Dolomites' location on the seafloor was pushed upward and folded due to the collision of the African and European plates. The Alps, a mountain range that stretches from Slovenia to France, were created by this process.

Different levels of height and exposure resulted from the Dolomites' gradual and uneven ascent. The Dolomites' higher portions were eroded by wind, water, and ice, while its lower portions were covered by sediments and shielded from weathering. The erosion chiseled out towers, pinnacles, spires, needles, and walls in the Dolomites, among other characteristic shapes and forms.

Ice Age, Quaternary Period

Repeated glaciations that left significant areas of the Earth covered in ice sheets during the Quaternary Period, which runs from 2.6 million years ago to the present, are what gave the period its name. The Ice Age also impacted the Dolomites, as glaciers moved forward and then backward through time. The glaciers sculpted the Dolomites' topography by creating valleys, cirques, moraines, and lakes. They also moved rocks and debris from higher to lower elevations, forming talus deposits and softer foothills.

The climate has been broadly steady and warm since the last glacier, which ended around 10,000 years ago. The Dolomites are now a large diversity of animals and plants that have evolved to varying ecosystems and altitudes. Human civilizations that have inhabited the Dolomites have contributed to the region's culture and history.

A World Heritage Site in the Present

The Dolomites are currently acknowledged as one of the world's most stunning and varied mountain ranges. They also contain a wealth of geological and biological knowledge that traces the evolution of life on Earth. In 2009, UNESCO designated the Dolomites as a World Heritage Site.

The nine components that make up the World Heritage for their exceptional natural beauty and scientific value ite span 141,903 hectares and safeguard numerous breathtaking ecosystems and landscapes

Millions of tourists who like hiking, skiing, climbing, cycling, and other activities go to the Dolomites each year as a significant tourist and pleasure destination. The Dolomites have inspired numerous writers, painters, photographers, and filmmakers who have expressed their admiration for their beauty and allure in various media.

The Dolomites physically represent our planet's lengthy and intricate past. They are gifts from the natural world that we must protect for future generations.

CHAPTER 1

PLANNING YOUR TRIP TO THE DOLOMITES

The Dolomites are a stunning destination for nature lovers, adventure seekers, and culture enthusiasts. They offer a variety of landscapes, activities, and attractions that will make your trip unforgettable. However, planning a trip to the Dolomites can be challenging, as there are many factors to consider, such as when to go, where to stay, how to get around, and what to see and do. In this guide, we will help you plan your perfect trip to the Dolomites, whether you have one day or five days.

When to Go

The best time to visit the Dolomites depends on what you want to do and see. The Dolomites have four distinct seasons, each with its advantages and disadvantages.

Spring (March to May): **This is an excellent time to enjoy the blooming flowers, green meadows, and mild temperatures. However, some hiking trails and cable cars may remain closed due to snow or maintenance. You may also encounter rain or fog in some areas.**

Summer (June to August): This is the peak season for hiking, biking, climbing, and other outdoor activities. The weather is warm and sunny, and the views are spectacular. However, this is also the busiest and most expensive time of the year so you may face crowds, traffic, and higher prices. You may also need to book your accommodation and activities in advance.

Autumn (September to November): This is a great time to enjoy the fall colors, crisp air, and fewer crowds. The weather is still pleasant, and most hiking trails and cable cars are open until late October. However, some facilities may start to close in November as the winter season approaches. You may also experience some rain or snow in higher altitudes.

Winter (December to February): This is the best time for skiing, snowshoeing, sledding, and other winter sports. The Dolomites have some of the best ski resorts in the world, with over 1,200 kilometers of slopes that are part of the Dolomiti Superski area. The scenery is also magical, with snow-covered peaks and forests. However, this is also a popular and expensive time of the year, so you may need to book your accommodation and ski passes in advance. You may also face cold temperatures and limited daylight.

Where to Stay

The Dolomites cover a large area with many towns and villages offering different accommodation types. Depending on your budget, preferences, and itinerary, you can choose from hotels, apartments, chalets, B&Bs, campsites, or mountain huts.

Some of the most popular places to stay in the Dolomites are:

Cortina d'Ampezzo: **A chic town that hosted the 1956 Winter Olympics and is a hub for hiking, biking, skiing, and shopping. It is located in the eastern Dolomites and is close to attractions such as Tre Cime di Lavaredo, Lago di Misurina, Cinque Torri, Lagazuoi, and Croda da Lago.**

Val Gardena: **A valley that offers access to the Sella Ronda, a circular ski route around the Sella Group. It is located in the western Dolomites and is composed of three towns: Ortisei (St. Ulrich), Santa Cristina (St. Christina), and Selva (Wolkenstein). It is close to attractions such as Alpe di Siusi (Seiser Alm), Puez-Odle Nature Park (Naturpark Puez-Geisler), Sassolungo (Langkofel), Seceda (Secëda), and Val di Funes (Villnößtal).**

Val di Fassa: **A valley with a strong Ladin culture and language. It is located in the western Dolomites and is composed of seven towns: Moena (Moéna), Soraga (Soraga),**

Vigo di Fassa (Vich de Fascia), Pozza di Fassa (Poza de Fascia), Mazzin (Mazin), Campitello di Fassa (Ciampedèl), and Canazei (Cianacèi). It is close to attractions such as Marmolada (Marmoleda), Sella Group (Grup de Sela), Sciliar-Catinaccio Nature Park (Naturpark Schlern-Rosengarten), Lago di Carezza (Karersee), and Passo Pordoi (Pordoijoch).

Val Badia: A valley that has a strong Ladin culture and language. It is located in the western Dolomites and is composed of six towns: Badia (Abtei), Corvara in Badia (Corvara), La Valle (Wengen), La Villa (Stern), San Cassiano (St. Kassian), and San Martino in Badia (St. Martin in Thurn). It is close to attractions such as Sella Group (Grup de Sela), Fanes-Sennes-Prags Nature Park (Naturpark Fanes-Sennes-Prags), Lagazuoi (Lagació), and Santa Croce (Heiligkreuzkofel).

How to Get Around

Driving is the most convenient way to navigate the Dolomites. Driving in the Dolomites allows you the independence and flexibility to travel at your own pace and access locations challenging to get to by public transportation. Major airports and cities, including Venice, Milan, Verona, Innsbruck, and Munich, offer automobile rentals. A legitimate driver's license, an international driving permit (if needed by your nation), and a credit card are all necessary. In addition, you'll have to pay for parking, petrol, and tolls.

Driving in the Dolomites can be challenging, as the roads are narrow, winding, steep, and sometimes busy. You will also encounter many hairpin turns, tunnels, bridges, and passes. You must drive carefully and attentively and respect the speed limits and traffic rules. It would help if you also were prepared for changing weather conditions and road closures.

You can also use public transport around the Dolomites to avoid driving. Buses are the primary forms of public transportation.

Trains and cable cars. Buses are the most common and convenient way to travel between towns and villages, as they cover most routes and have frequent schedules. Trains are more limited and slower, but they can be helpful for longer distances or connecting to other regions. Cable cars are essential for reaching higher altitudes and accessing hiking trails or ski slopes.

Public transport in the Dolomites is generally reliable, comfortable, and affordable. However, it can also be crowded, especially during peak seasons or events. You must also plan your itinerary carefully and check the timetables and connections in advance.

You can buy tickets from ticket offices, machines, or online. You can also buy a travel card such as the Mobilcard or the Dolomiti Supersummer Card that allows you to use unlimited public transport for a certain period.

What to See and Do

The Dolomites offer various attractions and activities for all tastes and interests. Whether looking for nature, culture, adventure, or relaxation, you will find something to suit your preferences.

Some of the best things to see and do in the Dolomites are:

Hiking: The Dolomites are a paradise for hikers of all levels and abilities. You can choose from hundreds of trails that range from easy walks to challenging climbs. You can also take in breathtaking vistas of the

mountains, valleys, lakes, forests, and meadows. Some of the best hiking trails in the Dolomites are Tre Cime di Lavaredo Loop (Drei Zinnen Rundweg), Alpe di Siusi Loop (Seiser Alm Rundweg), Seceda Ridgeline (Secëda Gratweg), Lago di Braies Circuit (Pragser Wildsee Rundweg), Croda da Lago Circuit (Croda da Lago Rundweg), Sassolungo Loop

(Langkofel Rundweg), Val di Funes Loop (Villnößtal Rundweg), Marmolada Glacier Trail (Marmoleda Gletscherweg), Lagazuoi Tunnels Trail (Lagació Tunnelweg), Cinque Torri Loop (Fünf Türme Rundweg).

Skiing: The Dolomites are one of the best skiing destinations in the world, with over 1,200 kilometers of slopes that are part of the Dolomiti Superski area. You can ski on different types of terrain, from gentle slopes to steep couloirs. Furthermore, you can enjoy beautiful views of the

snow-covered peaks and valleys. Some of the best ski resorts in the Dolomites are: Cortina d'Ampezzo (Queen of the Dolomites), Val Gardena (Gröden), Val di Fassa (Fassatal), Val Badia (Gadertal), Alta Badia (Hochabtei), Kronplatz (Plan de Corones), Arabba-Marmolada (Arabba-Marmoleda), San Martino di Castrozza-Passo Rolle (San Martino di Castrozza-Rollepass).

Climbing: The Dolomites are a mecca for climbers of all levels and styles. You can find thousands of routes on different rock formations, from towers to walls. You can also try via Ferrata (iron paths), which are protected routes with metal cables, ladders, and bridges that allow you.

Choosing the Right Accommodations in Dolomites

The Dolomites are an excellent destination for nature lovers, adventure seekers, and culture enthusiasts. They offer a variety of landscapes, activities, and attractions that will make your trip unforgettable. However, choosing suitable accommodations in the Dolomites can take time because there are many things to consider,

such as your budget, preferences, itinerary, and transportation. This guide will help you choose suitable accommodations in the Dolomites, whether you are looking for a luxurious chalet, a wellness retreat, a budget hostel, or a mountain hut.

Your Budget

The first factor to consider when choosing your accommodations in the Dolomites is your budget. The Dolomites are a costly destination, especially during peak seasons (summer and winter), when prices can be high and availability can be low. However, there are options for different budgets, from high-end hotels to affordable apartments.

Some of the most expensive places to stay in the Dolomites are:

Cortina d'Ampezzo: **A chic town known as the Queen of the Dolomites, offers elegant hotels, restaurants, and shops. It is also a hiking, biking, skiing, and shopping hub. Some of the best hotels in Cortina d'Ampezzo are: Cristallo Resort & Spa (5 stars), Grand Hotel Savoia (5 stars), Hotel de la Poste (4 stars), Hotel Ancora (4 stars).**

Val Gardena: **A valley that offers access to the Sella Ronda, a circular ski route around the Sella Group. It is composed of three towns: Ortisei (St. Ulrich), Santa Cristina (St. Christina), and Selva (Wolkenstein). Some of the best hotels in Val Gardena are Adler Spa Resort Dolomiti (5 stars), Alpenroyal Grand Hotel (5 stars), Hotel Tyrol (4 stars), and Hotel Grones (4 stars).**

Some of the most affordable places to stay in the Dolomites are:

Val di Fassa: **A valley with a strong Ladin culture and language. It is composed of seven towns: Moena (Moéna), Soraga (Soraga), Vigo di Fassa (Vich de Fascia), Pozza di Fassa (Poza de Fascia), Mazzin (Mazin), Campitello di Fassa (Ciampedèl), and Canazei (Cianacèi).**

Some of the best budget hotels in Val di Fassa are Hotel La Romantica (3 stars), Hotel Catinaccio Rosengarten (3 stars), Hotel Villa Rosella Park & Wellness (3 stars), Hotel Villa Agomer (2 stars).

Val Badia: A valley that has a strong Ladin culture and language. It is composed of six towns: Badia (Abtei), Corvara in Badia (Corvara), La Valle (Wengen), La Villa (Stern), San Cassiano (St. Kassian), and San Martino in Badia (St. Martin in Thurn). Some of the best budget hotels in Val Badia are Hotel Gran Paradiso (3 stars), Hotel Col Alto (3 stars), Hotel Antines (3 stars), and Hotel Pider (3 stars).

Your Preferences

The second factor to consider when choosing your accommodations in the Dolomites is your preferences. The Dolomites offer different accommodations catering to different tastes and needs. Whether looking for comfort, convenience, charm, or authenticity, you will find something to suit your preferences.

Some of the most comfortable places to stay in the Dolomites are:

Wellness centers: These hotels offer spa facilities and treatments, such as saunas, pools, massages, and beauty services.

They are ideal for relaxing and rejuvenating after exploring the mountains. Some of the best wellness centers in the Dolomites are Rosa Alpina Hotel & Spa Relais & Chateaux (5 stars) in San Cassiano; QC Terme Dolomiti (4 stars) in Pozza di Fassa; Lagació Mountain Residence & Spa (4 stars) in San Cassiano; My Arbor - Plose Wellness Hotel (4 stars) in Bressanone.

Chalets: These are cozy and rustic lodges that offer a home-away-from-home feeling. They are usually equipped with kitchens, fireplaces, balconies, and gardens. They are ideal for families or groups who want more space and privacy. Some of the best chalets in the Dolomites are Chalet Tofana - Mountain Living Hotel (4 stars) in San Cassiano; Chalet Elisabeth - Dolomites Alpin & Charme (4 stars) in Selva di Val Gardena; Chalet Vites Mountain Hotel (4 stars) in Canazei; Chalet Laura Lodge Hotel (4 stars) in Madonna di Campiglio.

Some of the most convenient places to stay in the Dolomites are:

Apartments: These are self-catering units that offer more flexibility and independence. They usually have kitchens, living rooms, bedrooms, and bathrooms. They are ideal for travelers who want to save money and cook meals. Some of the best apartments in the Dolomites are: Ciasa de Munt Lifestyle B&B (4 stars) in Corvara in Badia; Residence Villa Toni (3 stars) in Cortina d'Ampezzo; Residence Antares (3 stars) in Selva di Val Gardena; Residence Contrin (3 stars) in Canazei.

Mountain huts are simple and basic shelters offering a bed and a meal. They are usually located in remote and scenic locations along hiking trails or ski slopes. They are ideal for travelers who want to experience authentic mountain life and meet other hikers or skiers. Some of the best mountain huts in the Dolomites are Rifugio Lagazuoi (2 stars) on Lagazuoi Peak; Rifugio Averau (2 stars) near Cinque Torri; Rifugio Fanes (2 stars) in Fanes-Sennes-Prags Nature Park; Rifugio Puez (2 stars) in Puez-Odle Nature Park.

Your Itinerary

The third factor to consider when choosing your Dolomite accommodations is your itinerary. The Dolomites cover a large area with many Visits to these places, and engaging in these activities will be unforgettable. Depending on how many days you plan to spend in the Dolomites, where you plan to go, and what you plan to do, you can choose your accommodations accordingly.

Some of the best places to stay in the Dolomites for one day are:

Cortina d'Ampezzo: **If you only have one day in the Dolomites, Cortina d'Ampezzo is an excellent base to explore some of the region's highlights. You can visit Tre Cime di Lavaredo, Lago di Misurina, Cinque Torri, Lagazuoi, and Croda da Lago from here. You can also enjoy the town's atmosphere, shops, and restaurants.**

Val Gardena: **If you only have one day in the Dolomites, Val Gardena is another good base to explore some of the region's highlights. You can visit Alpe di Siusi, Puez-Odle Nature Park, Sassolungo, Seceda, and Val di Funes from here. You can also enjoy the valley's culture, cuisine, and crafts.**

Some of the best places to stay in the Dolomites for three days are:

Cortina d'Ampezzo and Val Gardena: **If you have three days in the Dolomites, you can split your time between Cortina d'Ampezzo and Val Gardena to see both the eastern and western parts of the region. You can spend one day in Cortina d'Ampezzo and visit Tre Cime di Lavaredo, Lago di Misurina, Cinque Torri, Lagazuoi, and Croda da Lago. You can spend another day in Val Gardena and visit Alpe di Siusi, Puez-Odle Nature Park, Sassolungo, Seceda, and Val di**

Funes. You can spend the third day driving between the two towns and stopping at other attractions, such as Lago di Braies, Passo Giau, Marmolada, or Sciliar-Catinaccio Nature Park.

Val di Fassa and Val Badia: If you have three days in the Dolomites, you can also split your time between Val di Fassa and Val Badia to see another side of the region. You can spend one day in Val di Fassa and visit Marmolada, Sella Group, Sciliar-Catinaccio Nature Park, Lago di Carezza, and Passo Pordoi. You can spend another day in Val Badia and visit Sella Group, Fanes-Sennes-Prags Nature Park, Lagazuoi, Santa Croce, and San Martino in Badia. You can spend the third day driving between the two valleys and stopping at other attractions, such as Passo Sella, Passo Gardena, or Passo Campolongo.

Packing List for the Dolomites

The Dolomites are a beautiful location for hiking, climbing, bicycling, and other outdoor activities. They provide a range of settings, vistas, and difficulties that will make your journey unforgettable. Packing for the Dolomites can be challenging, though, since you must be ready for various weather, altitude, and terrain conditions. Whether you are visiting the Dolomites for a day or a week, this packing list will assist you.

Essentials to Pack

No of the time of year or how long your trip will last, there are certain things you should always bring with you while visiting the Dolomites. As follows:

The most crucial piece of gear for the Dolomites is a pair of reliable, top-notch hiking boots. They should have a firm grip and support and be breathable, waterproof, and comfy. For walking on many types of trails, from simple paths to rough hills, you will require them. You might also need to carry your climbing shoes, depending on how much climbing you plan to do.

You'll need a backpack to transport your necessities on the trails. It should be portable, robust, and equipped with adequate compartments and capacity to meet your needs. It should be insulated with plastic or have a rain cover for added protection from snow and rain. A daypack carrying 20 to 30 liters is usually sufficient for day hikes, but longer trips, such as hut-to-hut treks, may call for a 40 to 60-liter backpack.

Water bottle: The Dolomites need constant hydration, especially at higher altitudes. Bring a refillable water bottle to fill it up at the mountain cabins, springs, or fountains you pass. If you are still determining the quality or availability of the water, you might also bring a water filter or purification tablets.

Sun protection: The sun may be extremely intense on the Dolomites, mainly when it reflects off the snow or the rocks. Sunglasses, sunscreen, lip balm, and a sun hat or buff should all be worn to prevent sunburns and sunstroke. You can also put on long sleeves and comfortable, breathable slacks to cover your skin.

A windbreaker is a necessity while visiting the Dolomites. Even on a beautiful day, you can experience strong gusts that leave you feeling chilly and unpleasant. You may add another layer of warmth and defense against the wind and rain by donning a windbreaker. It ought to be compact, watertight, and light.

First aid supplies On the Dolomites, you can never be sure when you'll need some basic medical supplies. Bring a first aid kit with bandages, gauze, antiseptic wipes, painkillers, anti-inflammatory medications, blister plasters, tweezers, scissors, and safety pins. You can also provide any personal medications or prescriptions you may require.

A compass and a map, even though most of the trails in the Dolomites are marked and simple to follow, it is always a good idea to carry a map and compass just in case you need to modify your course or become disoriented. Ensure you have enough battery life and signal before using a GPS gadget or an app. A guidebook or other information about the trails and sites you intend to see can be brought along or downloaded.

Tips for Packing In addition to the necessities, some suggestions might make your Dolomites packing more efficient and lighter. As follows:

Bring layers, as the weather in the Dolomites is prone to sudden and drastic changes depending on the time of year, the day, and the altitude. The valleys will be warm, and the summits will be frigid. Rain, snow, fog, and hail are all possible anytime. Layers you may add or remove as necessary should be packed to prepare for any weather scenario. Examples of coatings include:

Base layer: **This protects the surface of your skin and controls moisture and body temperature. Breathable, quick-**

drying, and odor-resistant fabrics should be used, such as synthetic or merino wool. Do not wear cotton because it takes longer to dry and absorbs sweat.

The middle layer is the one that offers warmth and insulation. Lightweight fleece or down textiles should be used to make it.

Dolomites Visa and Entry Requirements

The Schengen Area includes the Dolomites, a mountain range in the northern Italian Alps. This implies that visitors from other Schengen nations only need an ID card to enter Italy; neither a visa nor a passport is required. However, depending on their country, intended use, and duration of stay, visitors from outside the Schengen Area can need a visa.

Temporary visa

Travelers who intend to visit Italy for up to 90 days during 180 days for tourism, business, family, or cultural purposes must get a short-stay visa. Because it permits entry into additional Schengen nations, this visa is often known as a Schengen visa.

You can consult the database Visa for Italy1, which provides a list of visa requirements for various nations and purposes, to determine whether you need a short-stay visa for Italy. You can also view a list of countries without visa requirements on the same page.

Before your journey, you must apply for a short-stay visa at the Italian embassy or consulate in your home country. You must submit the following paperwork:

A current, ten-year-old passport or other acceptable travel document valid for at least three more months after the date you want to leave Schengen.

A fully filled-out and signed visa application.

A pair of current passport-size pictures.

A certification that your travel health insurance has at least €30,000 in emergency and repatriation coverage.

A document demonstrating your ability to stay in Italy, like a hotel reservation or a letter from your host inviting you.

A document demonstrates that you have the necessary proof of travel expenses, like a bank statement or sponsorship letter.

A document that serves as proof of your travel plans, like a round-trip ticket or a reservation confirmation.

A piece of evidence demonstrating the reason behind your travel, such as a letter of invitation from a friend or family member, a confirmation of enrollment in a class or event, or proof of involvement in a cultural activity.

You might also be required to submit other documents, such as a work permit, a study certificate, a marriage certificate, or parental consent, depending on the details of your situation. The Visa for Italy database1 has more information on the required documentation.

The visa charge is €40 for children under six and €80 for adults. Children under the age of six are not charged. The price may be eliminated or reduced for specific application categories, such as students, researchers, cultural workers, or family members of EU/EEA nationals.

A short-stay visa typically takes 15 days to process; however, in exceptional circumstances, that time frame may be increased to 60 days. Apply as early as 15 days, but no later than six months before the day you expect to travel.

Long-stay permit

Travelers who intend to stay in Italy for more than 90 days during 180 days, whether for job, study, family reunion, or residency, must get a long-stay visa. As it is given by the Italian authorities following their domestic law, this visa is also known as a national visa or a D-visa.

You can consult the database Visa for Italy1, which provides a list of visa criteria for various nations and purposes, to determine whether you need a long-stay visa for Italy. On the same page, you can also look for a list of countries with particular agreements with Italy.

If you want a long-stay visa, you must apply in advance of your travel at the Italian embassy or consulate in your home country. You must submit the following paperwork:

A current, ten-year-old passport or other acceptable travel document valid for at least three more months after the day you want to leave Italy.

A fully filled-out and signed visa application.

A pair of current passport-size pictures.

A certification that your travel health insurance has at least €30,000 in emergency and repatriation coverage.

A document proving lodgings in Italy, such as a lease agreement or a host's invitation letter.

A record of your ability to pay for your stay, such as a bank statement or a sponsorship letter.

A document proving your reason for staying, such as a letter of employment, a letter of enrollment in school, a certificate of family status, or a residence permit application.

You can also be required to submit other documents, such as an integration agreement, a criminal background certificate, a health certificate, or a certificate proving your ability to speak Italian. The Visa for Italy database1 has more details on the required documentation.

Visa costs €116 for adults and €58 for youngsters between 6 and 12. Children under the age of six are not charged. The price may be eliminated or reduced for specific application categories, such as students, researchers, cultural workers, or family members of EU/EEA nationals.

Depending on the kind and purpose of the visa, the processing time ranges from 30 to 120 days for long-stay tickets. You should submit your application as soon as possible but no later than six months beforehand.

entry prerequisites

Once you have your visa, you can enter Italy at any permitted entry point, including airports, seaports, and land borders.

At border check, you will be required to provide the following documents:

A current passport or other form of identification, and, if required, your visa sticker.

A statement confirming you have travel health insurance with a minimum of €30,000 in emergency and repatriation coverage.

A document demonstrating your ability to stay in Italy, like a hotel reservation or a letter from your host inviting you.

A statement from your bank or a letter from your sponsor proving you have the money you need for your trip.

A document that serves as proof of your travel plans, like a round-trip ticket or a reservation confirmation.

A record demonstrating the reason for your travel, such as an official letter of invitation from a friend or family member, proof of enrollment in a program or course, or evidence of involvement in a cultural engagement.

Additionally, the border agent could inquire about your visit to Italy and ask you things like:

Why are you going to Italy, exactly?

How much time do you plan to spend in Italy?

Where will you be staying in Italy?

The decision on whether or not to allow you access to Italy rests with the border agent. You will be granted admission and given a stamp on your passport if you satisfy all the entry conditions and don't endanger Italy. The logo shows the time and location of your entry and the length of your permitted stay.

Ensure you stay within the 90-day limit for visa-exempt travelers within a 180-day window. If you do, you could be subject to fines, deportation, or a future entry ban into Italy or the Schengen Area.

The Dolomites' money and language

The Southern Limestone Alps, of which the Dolomites are a part, is a northeastern Italy mountain range. They are a UNESCO World Heritage Site and a well-liked place to go cycling, climbing, hiking, and skiing. The Dolomites are found in three Italian regions: Veneto, Trentino-Alto Adige/Südtirol, and Friuli Venezia Giulia, as well as numerous of its provinces.

The euro (€), the official currency of Italy and 18 other members of the European Union is used in the Dolomites. In 2002, the Italian lira was phased out and replaced with the euro. One hundred cents are equal to one euro. There are eight different euro coin denominations, as well as seven additional euro currency denominations (€5, €10, €20, €50, €100, €200, and €500), including two cents, five cents, ten cents, twenty cents, fifty cents,

and 1 penny. In the Dolomites, numerous stores, eateries, hotels, and other businesses accept the euro.

Because of the historical and cultural impacts of various peoples and states over the centuries, the language situation in the Dolomites is complex and diverse. Italian, German, and Ladin are the main languages of the Dolomites. Italian is the most widely used language in the Dolomites and is the national tongue of Italy.

It belongs to the Romance branch of the Indo-European language family and has many regional dialects and varieties. Trentino-Alto Adige/Südtirol is one region that includes a portion of the Dolomites, and German is that region's official language.

Numerous varieties of this Indo-European language family are spoken in various valleys and cities. It is a member of the Germanic branch. About 30,000 people speak Ladin, a minority language, in the five Dolomite valleys of Val Gardena, Alta Badia, Cortina d'Ampezzo, Fodom, and Val di Fassa. It is a member of the Romance language family's

Rhaeto-Romance branch with several valley-specific variations.

The language of the Dolomites in antiquity, which eventually merged with Celtic, Germanic, and Slavic peoples, is descended from a vulgar Latin dialect known as ladin. Italy acknowledges Ladin as a protected language and has its own educational, media, and cultural institutions.

Other languages like Venetian, Friulian, Cimbrian, and Mcheno are also spoken by smaller villages or tribes in the Dolomites in addition to these three. These languages, each with histories, traits, and statuses, add to the Dolomites' linguistic diversity and richness.

The Dolomites' natural beauty and outdoor recreation are remarkable, but so are the region's rich cultural and linguistic traditions. Visitors can encounter several languages and cultures within a comparatively short area and learn about the locals' history and customs.

Budget advice for the Dolomites

Northeastern Italy's magnificent Dolomites mountain range is home to activities including cycling, climbing, skiing, and hiking among its craggy peaks and verdant valleys. However, going to the Dolomites is expensive because you must pay for lodging, meals, transportation, and activities.

Here are some recommendations and cost ranges to assist you in making your Dolomites travel budget.

Accommodation: The price of housing in the Dolomites varies depending on the season, location, type, and quality of the lodging. Generally, you can expect to pay at least €70 per night for an entry-level hotel or guesthouse or more if you want a higher standard or a better view. If you are on a tight budget, you can opt for camping or bivouacking, which can cost around €10 to €20 per night per person. Alternatively, you can stay in mountain huts or rifugios, basic but cozy shelters offering beds, meals, and facilities for hikers and skiers. The price of a rifugio ranges from €20 to €50 per night per person, depending on whether you choose a dormitory or a private room, and includes breakfast and dinner.

Food: Food is another significant expense to consider when visiting the Dolomites. You can save money by cooking meals by accessing a kitchen or camping equipment or buying snacks and sandwiches from supermarkets or bakeries. However, if you want to try the local cuisine, a mix of Italian, German, and Ladin influences, you must budget for restaurants and cafes. A typical meal in a restaurant can cost between €15 and €30 per person, depending on the type of dish and the location. For example, a pizza or pasta dish can be cheaper than a meat or cheese platter.

A coffee or a drink can cost between €1 and €5, depending on whether you sit at the bar or a table. A tip of 10% is usually expected in restaurants and cafes

Transport: Transport is another major cost factor when visiting the Dolomites. The most convenient and flexible way to get around the Dolomites is by car, as you can reach most places easily and quickly. However, renting a car can be expensive, especially in high season. Depending on the vehicle's size and model, you can anticipate paying between €40 and €80 per day for a rental car. Additional costs include:

Gasoline (approximately €1.6 per liter).

Parking (about €1.5 per hour).

Some highway tolls (about €10 to €20 for each journey).

Insurance (optional but advised).

Alternatively, you can travel to the Dolomites via public transportation, comprising buses and trains that link the major towns and valleys. Bus tickets can cost between €1 and €5, depending on the route and destination. Depending on the same factors, the cost of a single rail ticket may range from €2 to €10. You can also buy a travel card that entitles you to limitless public transit usage for a predetermined period (for example, €28 for seven days).

Public transit could be less regular, dependable, and uncomfortable than driving a car, though, particularly in remote areas or during bad weather.

Activities: The Dolomites offer a wide range of activities for outdoor enthusiasts of all levels and interests. You can hike on numerous trails that vary in difficulty, duration, and scenery, from easy walks to challenging climbs. You can ski on some of the best slopes in Europe, with over 1200 km of pistes and 450 lifts. You can cycle on scenic roads or mountain bike trails that test your skills and stamina.

You can also try other sports, such as rock climbing via Ferrata (iron paths), paragliding, rafting, or horse riding. The cost of these activities depends on whether you need to rent equipment, hire a guide or instructor, buy a lift pass, or pay an entrance fee.

For example, renting ski equipment can cost between €15 and €30 per day per person; hiring a ski instructor can cost between €40 and €80 per hour; buying a ski pass can cost between €40 and €60 per day per person; renting a bike can cost between €10 and €30 per day; hiring a bike guide can cost between €50 and €100 per day; doing a via ferrata can cost between €50 and €100 per person; paragliding can cost between €100 and €150 per person; rafting can cost between €40 and €60 per person; horse riding can cost between €20 and €40 per hour

The Dolomites are an excellent destination for nature lovers but are costly. A suggested budget for the Dolomites is around €1400 for a week for two people, or €100 per day per person, assuming you stay in a basic hotel, eat in restaurants, rent a car and do some activities. Of course, you can adjust this budget according to your preferences, needs, and travel style. You can spend more if you want more comfort, luxury, or adventure or less if you are willing to compromise, save or improvise. The most important thing is to enjoy the beauty and charm of the Dolomites!

Dolomites money-saving advice:

The Dolomites are a great vacation destination for those who enjoy the outdoors, but they can also be extremely pricey, especially during the summer. Without sacrificing the caliber of your trip, numerous methods exist to cut costs and take in the Dolomites. To visit the Dolomites affordably, consider the following advice:

Traveling in the off-peak or shoulder season is recommended because July and August are warm and sunny. December and January, when the ski resorts are open, are the busiest and most expensive months to visit the Dolomites. Consider traveling during off-peak or shoulder seasons like May, June, September, or October to escape the lines and costly expenses. More availability and flexibility, as well as less expensive lodging, travel, and auto rentals, are all available.

The landscape's shifting hues, from springtime blooms to autumnal foliage, will likewise be pleasing to the eye. When visiting in the off-season, remember that some attractions, services, and facilities can be limited or closed.

Be discerning when choosing your lodging: One of the most significant costs when traveling through the Dolomites is lodging, particularly if you want to book a room in a hotel or guesthouse with a view. Alternatives exist, though, so you can still have a comfortable trip while saving money. Camping or bivouacking, for instance, might cost between €10 and €20 per night per person.

Rifugios, which are simple but comfortable lodgings that provide beds, meals, and amenities for hikers and skiers, is another accommodation option. Depending on whether you select a shared or private room and whether you choose to include breakfast and dinner, the cost of a rifugio ranges from €20 to €50 per night per person.

If you travel in a group or with a family, staying in an apartment or vacation home may be more affordable than a hotel. Additionally, making your food will save you money.

Meals. On websites like Booking.com or Airbnb, you may find flats and vacation rentals.

Eat sensibly: Food is yet another price to consider when traveling to the Dolomites. If you can access a kitchen or camping gear, you can save money by preparing meals. Otherwise, you can spend less money purchasing sandwiches and snacks from bakeries or supermarkets. You must set aside money for restaurants and cafes to sample the regional food, which combines elements from Italian, German, and Ladin cultures.

According to the type of cuisine and the location, the average restaurant dinner can cost between €15 and €30 per person. An alternative to a meat or cheese plate can be a pizza or pasta meal. Depending on where you sit—at the bar or a table—a coffee or other beverage may cost anywhere from €1 to €5. In restaurants and cafes, a standard gratuity is 10%. You can use the advice below to cut costs on food: dine during lunchtime rather than dinnertime when prices are lower; seek out eateries with a set menu or a daily special; stay away from touristy places and go where the locals go; consume takeout rather than a home meal; Bring your water bottle and fill it up at public fountains. Pack a picnic lunch for days you go trekking. Treat yourself to ice cream for dessert.

Share a car or take public transportation: Another significant expenditure when traveling to the Dolomites is transportation. Driving allows you to get to most locations quickly and easily, making it the most convenient and versatile option to travel across the Dolomites. But automobile rentals may be pricey, particularly during the summer.

Depending on the dimensions and make of the car, daily automobile rental costs typically range from €40 to €80. Additionally, you'll have to pay for gas ($1.6 per gallon), parking ($1.5 per hour), some highway tolls ($10 to $20 for each journey), and insurance ($optional but advised).

You can use these suggestions to reduce the cost of renting a car: Make your reservations early and shop around online; select a smaller, more fuel-efficient vehicle; stay away from airport rental agencies; return the car with a full tank; and, if at all possible, split the cost of the vehicle with other road trippers.

If you like, you can travel to the Dolomites via the buses and trains that connect the major towns and valleys. Depending on the route and destination, a single bus ticket may cost between €1 and €5. Depending on the same variables, one train ticket may cost between €2 and €10.

For a specific price (for instance, €28 for a week), you can also purchase a travel card that grants you unrestricted use of public transportation. But, especially in distant places or during severe weather, public transportation might be less frequent, less dependable, and less comfortable than driving a car.

Be selective with your activities: The Dolomites have a vast selection of activities for outdoor enthusiasts of all experience levels and interests. There are many routes where you can go hiking, ranging from simple strolls to strenuous climbs, and they differ in length, difficulty, and scenery.

With more than 1200 km of pistes and 450 lifts, the area offers some of the best skiing in Europe. Cycling is possible on attractive roads or challenging mountain bike tracks. Other sports you can participate in include horseback riding, rafting, paragliding, rock climbing, and ferrata (iron trails).

Whether you must pay an admission fee, rent equipment, hire a guide or teacher, purchase a lift pass, or pay a guide or instructor fee will determine how much these activities will cost.

For instance, renting ski equipment can cost between €15 and €30 per day per person, hiring a ski instructor can cost between €40 and €80 per hour, and purchasing a ski pass can cost between €40 and €60 per day per person. Renting a bike can cost between €10 and €30 per day, and hiring a bike guide can cost between €50 and €100 per day. Participating in an activity like a via Ferrata can cost between €50 and €100 per person, paraglide.

You can follow this advice to cut costs on activities: Look for discounts or bundles for several exercises or group reservations; pick free or inexpensive activities like hiking, swimming, or sightseeing; if you can, reserve online or beforehand; if you have your own, bring it with you; Avoid busy times and seasons when rates are higher; take a group trip or activity rather than a solo one.

CHAPTER 2

TOP ATTRACTIONS IN THE DOLOMITES

Go hiking

The Dolomites offer countless hiking trails for all levels of difficulty and fitness. The Tre Cime di Lavaredo loop, the Alpe di Siusi plateau, the Seceda ridge, and the Lago di Sorapis circuit are some of the most popular hikes.

Visit the lovely lakes

The Dolomites are home to some of Europe's most beautiful alpine lakes, such as Lago di Braies, Lago Federa, Lago di Misurina, and Lago di Carezza. These lakes have crystal-clear water and reflect the surrounding mountains in stunning colors.

Drive the mountain passes

The Dolomites have some of the most scenic roads in the world, winding through spectacular landscapes and offering breathtaking views. Some of the best mountain passes to drive are the Passo Pordoi, the Sella Pass, the Passo Giau, and the Gardena Pass.

Visit Alpe di Siusi (Seiser Alm). Alpe di Siusi is the largest alpine meadow in Europe, covering an area of 56 square kilometers. It is a great place to enjoy nature, admire the views of the Sassolungo and Sciliar massifs, and spot wildlife such as marmots, deer, and cows.

Visit Val di Funes

Val di Funes is a picturesque valley in the Dolomites, famous for its iconic views of the Geisler (Odle) peaks and the charming churches of Santa Maddalena and San Giovanni. It is a peaceful and relaxing place to explore by foot or by bike.

Ride the Freccia nel Cielo Cable Car to Cima Tofana.

Cima Tofana is one of the highest peaks in the Dolomites, reaching 3244 meters above sea level. You can get it by taking the Freccia nel Cielo cable car from Cortina d'Ampezzo, which has spectacular views of the valleys and mountains. At the top, you can enjoy a panoramic terrace, a restaurant, and a museum dedicated to mountaineering.

Ride the Cable Car to Seceda

Seceda is another impressive peak in the Dolomites, with a dramatic vertical wall that drops 2500 meters to the valley below. You can access it via cable car from Ortisei or Santa Cristina in Val Gardena.

At the top, you can admire one of the most iconic views in the Dolomites, hike along the ridge, or visit a cross-shaped monument commemorating fallen soldiers.

Ski or snowboard

The Dolomites are a winter wonderland for skiers and snowboarders, with hundreds of kilometers of slopes, modern lifts, and cozy huts. The most famous ski area is the Sella Ronda, a circular route that connects four valleys: Val Gardena, Alta Badia, Val di Fassa, and Arabba.

CHAPTER 3

DOLOMITES BEST RESTAURANTS AND CAFÉS

The Dolomites have a rich and varied culinary scene, influenced by the Italian, Austrian, and Ladin cultures. Many restaurants and cafés serve delicious dishes, from pizza and pasta to meat and cheese, from strudel and tiramisu to apple pie and ice cream. Here are some of the best restaurants and cafés in the Dolomites that you should try:

Rifugio Laresei

This cozy mountain hut is located at the top of Cima Pradazzo, accessible by a chairlift from Falcade. It offers traditional dishes such as polenta, cheese, sausages, goulash, homemade desserts, and grappa. The views from the terrace are stunning.

L'Ostaria da Besic

This popular restaurant and pizzeria in the centre of Canazei has a wooden interior and a friendly atmosphere. It serves a variety of pizzas, pasta, burgers, grilled meat, and local specialties such as canederli (bread dumplings) and casunziei (ravioli). The portions are generous, and the prices are reasonable.

Baita Cuca Hutte

This is a charming alpine hut near Santa Cristina Valgardena, with a panoramic view of the Sassolungo mountain. It serves authentic Tyrolean cuisine, such as speck (smoked ham), knödel (dumplings), kaiserschmarrn (shredded pancake), and apfelstrudel (apple strudel). The staff are friendly, and the atmosphere is cozy.

Turonda PIZZA-Bistrot-Drinks

This modern and stylish restaurant and bar in Ortisei has a spacious terrace and a lively vibe. It specializes in pizza, made with organic flour and fresh ingredients, and offers salads, sandwiches, burgers, and desserts. The drinks menu includes cocktails, wines, beers, and juices.

Restaurant Terra

This fine dining restaurant in Sarentino has a Michelin star and a Slow Food certification. It serves creative and refined dishes inspired by local products and traditions, such as trout tartare, lamb loin, buckwheat gnocchi, and chocolate cake. The service is flawless, and the wine list is broad.

Pasticceria della Nonna

This family-run pastry shop and café in Peio Fonti has a cozy interior and a sunny terrace. It offers a wide selection of cakes, pastries, cookies, chocolates, and ice cream, all made with natural ingredients and love. Additionally, you can indulge in coffee, tea, hot or fresh juice.

Traditional Restaurants In The Dolomites

El Molin

This is a Michelin-starred restaurant in an old mill in Cavalese. It serves elegant and sophisticated dishes, such as trout tartare, lamb loin, buckwheat gnocchi, and chocolate cake. The service is flawless, and the wine list is broad.

Durnwald

This family-run restaurant in the Val di Casies has a cozy and rustic atmosphere. It specializes in ultra-fresh, locally sourced seasonal South Tyrolean cuisine, such as speck (smoked ham), knödel (dumplings), kaiserschmarrn (shredded pancake), and apfelstrudel (apple strudel).

Prè de Costa.

This is a farm-to-table restaurant in an old barn near Fiera di Primiero. It serves authentic and delicious dishes like polenta, cheese, sausages, goulash, and homemade desserts. The views from the terrace are stunning.

Gostner Schwaige

This is a mountain hut on the Alpe di Siusi, with a panoramic view of the Sassolungo mountain. It serves creative and refined dishes, such as cheese soup with truffles, nettle dumplings with butter and sage, and blueberry pie with vanilla ice cream. The chef also makes his flavoured grappas.

Rifugio Fanes

This is a welcoming oasis in the heart of the mountains near San Vigilio di Marebbe. It serves traditional and tasty dishes, such as barley soup, canederli (bread dumplings), casunziei (ravioli stuffed with pumpkin or spinach), and krapfen (fried doughnuts). The staff are friendly, and the atmosphere is cozy.

Restaurant Ladinia

This is a cozy and elegant restaurant in Corvara in Badia. It serves mountain-style food with a modern twist, such as smoked trout salad, venison ragout with polenta, and apple pie with cinnamon ice cream. The wine list is impressive, and the service is attentive.

Costamula

This charming alpine hut near Canazei has a wooden interior and fireplace. It serves authentic and hearty dishes like cheese fondue, grilled meat, mushroom risotto, and tiramisu. The portions are generous, and the prices are reasonable.

La Siriola

This fine dining restaurant near San Cassiano has two Michelin stars and a Slow Food certification. It serves creative and refined dishes inspired by local products and traditions, such as trout tartare with horseradish cream, lamb loin with artichokes and mint sauce, and chocolate cake with raspberry sorbet. Both the wine list and the service are extensive.

Acherer Patisserie & Blumen.

This family-run pastry shop and café near Brunico has a cozy interior and sunny terrace. It offers a wide selection of cakes, pastries, cookies, chocolates, and ice cream, all made with natural ingredients and love. Additionally, you can sip on hot chocolate, coffee, tea, or fresh juice.

St Hubertus

This is a quietly elegant foodie destination near San Cassiano, with three Michelin stars. It serves exquisite dishes that showcase the best local ingredients, such as mountain beef cooked in hay with herb sauce, potato gnocchi with porcini mushrooms and black truffle sauce, and raspberry soufflé with vanilla sauce.

International cuisine in the Dolomites

Restaurant Terra in Sarentino: This restaurant serves Italian and European dishes made from local farms with fresh and organic ingredients. Seasonal changes affect the food and the availability of the products. You can enjoy a panoramic view of the mountains while dining in a cosy and elegant atmosphere.

HERO La Casa del Burger in Predazzo: This place specializes in burgers, not just burgers. They use high-quality meat from local farms, homemade bread and sauces, and various toppings and cheeses. There are also vegetarian and vegan choices available.

And salads, fries and desserts. The restaurant has a modern and colourful decor inspired by comic books and superheroes.

Baita Cuca Hutte in Santa Cristina Valgardena: This traditional alpine hut is 2,100 meters above sea level. You can reach it by cable car or by hiking. The hut serves Italian and Austrian dishes, such as dumplings, goulash, strudel and kaiserschmarrn. You can also enjoy a glass of schnapps or mulled wine while admiring the view of the Sassolungo mountain.

These are just some of the many restaurants that offer international cuisine in the Dolomites.

Cafés And Bakeries In The Dolomites

I Dolci di Ricky in Badia: **This is a family-run bakery that makes homemade strudels, cakes, pies, croissants and more. Additionally, you can sip on some coffee,**

 tea or hot chocolate while admiring the view of the mountains. The bakery is open every day from 7 am to 7 pm.

Caffe Val d'Anna in Ortisei: **This is a cosy and rustic café that serves Italian and international dishes, such as salads, sandwiches, soups, pasta and pizza. You can also try their desserts, such as tiramisu, apple pie or cheesecake. The café is next to a ski slope and has a large terrace to relax and enjoy the sun.**

Caffe Adler in Ortisei: **This historic café dates back to 1810. It offers a wide selection of coffee, tea, hot chocolate and herbal infusions. You can also taste their pastries, such as sacher torte, linzer torte or krapfen. The café has an elegant and refined atmosphere, with paintings and sculptures on the walls.

CHAPTER 4

THE DOLOMITES' NIGHTLIFE AND ENTERTAINMENT

A mountain range in northern Italy is called the Dolomites. Famous for its stunning scenery and outdoor activities. But they also offer fun and lively places to enjoy a drink, a dance or a show after dark. Here are some examples of nightlife and entertainment venues that you can find in the Dolomites:

Luislkeller in Selva di Val Gardena: This legendary après-ski pub attracts crowds of skiers and snowboarders with its loud music, friendly staff and humping rabbits logo. You can have a beer, a cocktail, or a shot while dancing to the DJ's music or singing along to folk melodies. Every day between 4 pm and 2 am, the pub is open.

L Rujin in Pozza di Fassa: This is a cosy and warm bar that serves delicious food and drinks in a rustic atmosphere. You can try their local specialities, such as cheese, salami, polenta and goulash, or their international dishes, such as burgers, pizzas and salads. In addition, you can sip grappa, wine, or coffee while watching sports on television or listening to live music. Every day from 8 am until 2 am, the bar is open.

Caffe Adler in Ortisei: This historic café dates back to 1810. It offers a wide selection of coffee, tea, hot chocolate and herbal infusions. You can also taste their pastries, such as sacher torte, linzer torte or krapfen. The café has an elegant and refined atmosphere, with paintings and sculptures on the walls. It also hosts cultural events, such as exhibitions, concerts and readings. The café is open every day from 7 am to 11 pm.

Dolomites bars and nightclubs:

Northern Italy's Dolomites mountain range is renowned for its breathtaking landscape, recreational activities, and vibrant culture. The Dolomites, however, offer a dynamic nightlife scene for anyone looking to have some fun after dark and are a popular destination for nature lovers and explorers. There are many places to choose from in the Dolomites, whether you're searching for a quiet wine bar, a buzzing pub, or a hip club.

Rifugio Piz Sorega, a pub and restaurant at the top of the Piz Sorega gondola in San Cassiano, is one of the most well-known places for nightlife in the Dolomites. This restaurant offers a fantastic view of the mountains, a comprehensive food selection, and a fun atmosphere.

You can enjoy a drink or dance with friends while listening to live music, DJ sets, fire pits, and visual projections2. You can visit Rifugio Piz Sorega any day or night because it is open from 9 am to 11:45 pm.

A renowned après-ski bar in Ortisei named Luislkeller is another well-known nightlife destination in the Dolomites1. This business has been running for over 40 years, and people recognize it by its emblem of humping bunnies on skis4. The welcoming staff, the cosiness of the decor, and loud Europop music all characterize Luislkeller. If a well-known folk song starts playing, you can join the residents and visitors who wave their napkins in the air4. You can visit Luislkeller after a long day on the slopes or remain till late because it's open from 4 pm to 2 am.

Venus is a chic wine bar in Bolzano that you should check out if you want something more refined and pleasant. This restaurant offers a sizable selection of wines by the glass in a dim, low-ceilinged setting. The proprietor, Peter, also offers a nightly tavola calda (a small hot menu) where you can order some delectable dishes2. You can have a relaxed nightcap or a romantic dinner at Venus because it's open from 6 pm to 1 am.

Kusk La Locanda is a fantastic choice for individuals who wish to dance the night away. Canazei-based establishment has four distinct sections: pizzeria, American bar, trash disco, and Italian restaurant1. You can select your preferred musical mood, such as rock, techno, or pop. From 6 pm until 3 am, Kusk La Locanda is open, allowing you to enjoy an entire evening of entertainment.

These are just a few of the countless bars and clubs in the Dolomites. Whatever your taste or price range, you will find something in this fantastic area that suits you. The Dolomites are a great spot to enjoy yourself and create lasting experiences in addition to admiring beauty and culture.

Places To Hear Live Music In The Dolomites

The Dolomites are a haven for music lovers, hikers, skiers, and climbers. The Sounds of the Dolomites is one of the most distinctive music festivals in the world, and it takes place every year in the Dolomites from August to October.

This festival brings together musicians from many genres and backgrounds in the open air, surrounded by the breathtaking Dolomites peaks and valleys. The event offers an opportunity to enjoy both uniquely and unforgettably as it celebrates music and nature.

The Trentino region, where the Dolomites are located, is home to the 17 concerts that comprise the Sounds of the Dolomites festival2. The venues are picked for their aesthetic value and accessibility, and they're typically close to huts or refuges where guests may unwind with a meal or beverage before or after the event.

Except for one exceptional event that begins at sunrise and provides a spectacular view of the first light of the day over the mountains, the concerts all begin at midday.

Jazz, classical, world music, folk, and pop musicians are among those who will perform at the event. Artists have played at previous events, including Paolo Fresu, Ludovico Einaudi, Avion Travel, Daniele Groff, Vinicio Capossela, Stefano Bollani, and many others.

A warm and relaxed atmosphere is produced by the artists' frequent interactions with the audience and one another. The Dolomites' inherent acoustics enhance the music, resulting in a pleasing mingling of noise and calm.

The audience must follow well-indicated routes or take guided walks with mountain guides from Trentino to see the concerts. The length and complexity of the hikes vary depending on where the concert will be held.

Others are more difficult and demand solid physical conditions, while some are simple and appropriate for families and kids.

The festival's experience includes the walks because they allow attendees to learn about the beauty and diversity of the Dolomites' scenery. The event also features trekking days where attendees may spend more time outside and interact with the performers.

The Sounds of the Dolomites event offers a singular chance to appreciate nature and music in one of the most breathtaking settings on earth. Everyone who enjoys music and mountains is welcome to attend the festival, which is free.

It is a chance to appreciate the Dolomites as a living, inspiring setting for art and culture and their status as a UNESCO World Heritage Site.

Dolomite Theatres And Performances

Various theatres and performances that appeal to various tastes and interests are available in the Dolomites. You may find it in the Dolomites, no matter what type of entertainment you are searching for—classical music, modern dance, comedy, or drama.

The Teatro Comunale di Bolzano, the city theatre of Bolzano, is one of the most known theatres in the Dolomites1. This theatre has 800 seats and was constructed in 1808. It features opera, ballet, musical, and theatre acts throughout the year.

Well-known performers, including Rudolf Nureyev, Maria Callas, Luciano Pavarotti, and Roberto Benigni, have all performed here. Additionally, the theatre hosts festivals, educational events, and guided tours.

The Teatro Zandonai di Rovereto, also known as the Zandonai Theater of Rovereto, is another well-known theatre in the Dolomites. There are 600 seats available in this theatre, which opened its doors in 1786. It bears the name of Rovereto-born composer Riccardo Zandonai.

The theatre presents performances by regional and international performers in concerts, operas, ballets, and plays. It also contains a museum where artefacts from the theatre's past, including costumes, instruments, and souvenirs, are displayed.

You should check out the Drodesera Festival, a contemporary performing arts festival held every summer in Dro, if you're seeking more unconventional and avant-garde performances. Since its founding in 1981, this festival has grown to rank among Italy's most significant occasions.

It exhibits experimental artwork created by up-and-coming and seasoned artists across various media, including theatre, dance, music, video art, and installation art. The festival is held in various locations, including a former factory, an ancient hydroelectric power station, and a natural park.

The Dolomites have several theatres and performing venues, to name a few. This area has many possibilities to explore and take advantage of. The Dolomites are a cultural centre for their richness and inventiveness in art and natural beauty, making them a UNESCO World Heritage Site.

CHAPTER 5

IN THE DOLOMITES, SHOPPING

Shopping enthusiasts will appreciate the Dolomites since they provide a wide range of goods and activities that capture the area's spirit, heritage and natural beauty. The Dolomites provide something to suit every taste and price range, whether you're seeking trinkets, handmade goods, food, wine, or clothing.

The Dolomites are known for their wood carving, a traditional art form that dates back to the 17th century and is one of their most well-known exports—using regional woods like pine, larch, and walnut, the wood carvers of the Dolomites craft exquisite sculptures of animals, religious figures, nativity scenes, and more. The towns and villages of the Dolomites, particularly in Val Gardena and Ortisei, are home to many stores and businesses that offer wood carvings1. Ciajea Woodcarvings, Albert Demetz Kunsthandwerk, and Artigiani Atesini are a few of the top shops to purchase wood carvings.

The speck, a smoked ham cured with salt, herbs, and spices, is another typical Dolomite product. A speck is one of the main ingredients in many regional meals, such as canederli (bread dumplings), spaghetti, and sandwiches.

Il Maso dello Speck, Butega Dal Vin Graus, and Latteria 3 Cime - Mondolatte are just a few of the many stores and markets where you can get speck in the Dolomites.

Try the strudel, a pastry stuffed with apples, raisins, almonds, and cinnamon, if you're craving something sweet. Strudel is a popular delicacy at bakeries and cafes all around the Dolomites. Peter's Tea House, Panificio Pulin, and Bread and Strudel Market are some top locations to purchase strudel.

Wine enthusiasts will discover various wines in the Dolomites that reflect the variety of the terrain and climate. The Trentino DOC and the Alto Adige DOC, which offer red wines like Lagrein, Teroldego, and Schiava, as well as white wines like Pinot Grigio, Chardonnay, and Gewürztraminer, are the two most well-known wine regions in the Dolomites. Many stores and wineries in the Dolomites, including Enoteca di Corso, La Salumeria Lunelli, and Vinus, sell these wines.

The Dolomites have a wide selection of stores that sell clothes, accessories, jewellery, and other fashion-related items. You can buy lederhosen, caps, jackets, dresses, and other Tyrolean fashion items from regional and worldwide apparel manufacturers. Via dei Portici, Franz Kraler, and

Galleria Doris Ghetta are a few of the top locations in the Dolomites for fashion shopping.

These are a few examples of the shopping options in the Dolomites. This area has many possibilities to explore and take advantage of. The Dolomites are an excellent destination for shopping and admiring beauty and culture.

Gifts and souvenirs in the Dolomites:

Wood carving, a traditional art form practised in this region for centuries, is one of the most recognizable memories of the Dolomites. Beautiful sculptures of animals, religious figures, nativity scenes, and other subjects are carved by local woodworkers in the Dolomites using regional woods like pine, larch, and walnut.

In numerous stores and workshops across the cities and villages of the Dolomites, particularly in Val Gardena and Ortisei, you may discover wood carvings of all sizes, designs, and price ranges. Artigiani Atesini, Ciajea Woodcarvings, and Albert Demetz Kunsthandwerk are a few of the most fabulous shops to purchase wood carvings.

Additionally, you can go to the Museum Gherdina in Ortisei, which features a variety of antique and modern wood sculptures from the Dolomites.

The speck, a smoked ham cured with salt, herbs, and spices, is another souvenir that embodies the culture and cuisine of the Dolomites.

A speck is one of the main ingredients in many regional meals, such as canederli (bread dumplings), spaghetti, and sandwiches. Il Maso dello Speck, Butega Dal Vin Graus, and Latteria Cime - Mondolatte are just a few of the Dolomites' stores and markets where you may get speck. In Funes, there is a Speck Museum where you can learn about this treat's background and culinary secrets.

The strudel, a pastry stuffed with apples, raisins, almonds, and cinnamon, will satisfy your sweet taste. Strudel is a popular delicacy at bakeries and cafes all around the Dolomites. Peter's Tea House, Panificio Pulin, and Bread and Strudel Market are some top locations to purchase strudel.

Additionally, the Strudel Academy in Bressanone offers classes with pastry chefs where you may learn how to make your strudel and then consume it.

Wine enthusiasts will discover a variety of wines in the Dolomites that reflect the variety of the terrain and climate. The Trentino DOC and the Alto Adige DOC, which offer red wines like Lagrein, Teroldego, and Schiava, as well as white wines like Pinot Grigio, Chardonnay, and Gewürztraminer, are the two most well-known wine regions in the Dolomites. Many stores and wineries in the Dolomites, including Enoteca di Corso, La Salumeria Lunelli, and Vinus, sell these wines.

At some of the top wineries in the area, like Cantina Tramin, Alois Lageder, and Ferrari Trento, you may also take part in a wine tour or tasting.

The Dolomites have a wide selection of stores that sell clothes, accessories, jewellery, and other fashion-related items. You can buy lederhosen, caps, jackets, dresses, and other Tyrolean fashion items from regional and worldwide apparel manufacturers.

Via dei Portici, Franz Kraler, and Galleria Doris Ghetta are a few of the top locations in the Dolomites for fashion shopping. Additionally, you can visit some regional markets that provide handmade things like candles, leather goods, ceramics, and more. Christkindlmarkt in Bolzano, Piazza Alessandro Vittoria in Trento, and Piazza della Vittoria in Bressanone are a few of the top markets in the Dolomites.

These are just a few illustrations of the presents and souvenirs you can purchase in the Dolomites. This area has many possibilities to explore and take advantage of. The

Dolomites are an excellent destination for shopping and admiring beauty and culture.

The Dolomites' Attire And Accessories

In addition to enjoying nature, sports, and cuisine, the Dolomites are also a great location to find clothing and accessories that capture the region's unique sense of style, history, and innovation. The Dolomites are the perfect place to shop for casual, sporty, or beautiful clothing that matches your style and situation.

Tyrolean-style apparel, which includes hats, jackets, gowns, and lederhosen, is one of the most distinct Dolomite fashion pieces. These clothes are constructed of wool, felt, or linen and have feathers, buttons, or embroidery. Both locals and visitors alike wear them, particularly during festivals and celebrations. In the Dolomites, you may find Tyrolean-inspired apparel in various stores and marketplaces, including Schafer, Romantik, and Rustikal - Mussner Andreas.

Sportswear, which comprises apparel, shoes, and accessories for hiking, skiing, cycling, and other outdoor activities, is another well-liked trend in the Dolomites. In addition to being attractive and current, these things are made to be practical, long-lasting, and comfy. Numerous stores and boutiques in the Dolomites, including Gary's Fashion & Sportswear, Ski Nives, and Boutique Pure Fashion, carry sportswear from regional and international companies.

Check out the designer clothing, including apparel, bags, shoes, and accessories from renowned Italian and worldwide designers, if you're seeking something more refined and elegant. These goods have distinctive designs and patterns and are made of premium fabrics and materials. Some of the Dolomites' most upscale stores and galleries, including Franz Kraler, Galleria Doris Ghetta, and Via dei Portici, carry designer clothing.

These are only a few illustrations of clothing and accessories you can discover in the Dolomites. This area has many possibilities to explore and take advantage of. The Dolomites are a location to express your sense of style and taste in addition to admiring nature and culture.

The Dolomites' Food and Drink

Northern Italy's magnificent Dolomites mountain range is known for its craggy peaks, picturesque valleys, and vibrant culture. But the Dolomites are also a culinary and beverage lover's dream, offering a wide selection of meals and drinks that pay homage to the region's culture, history, and geography. I'll discuss some of the most popular and delectable foods and beverages in the Dolomites in this post and why you should try them.

the impact of three different cultures

The fact that the Italian, German, and Ladin cultures have all impacted the food and drink in the Dolomites is one of its most intriguing features. Pasta, cheese, wine, and olive oil are often used in Italian cuisine, and fresh and in-season items are preferred.

In addition to the hearty and meat-based recipes, the German influence may be noticed in the consumption of bread, dumplings, sausages, beer, and schnapps. The earliest influence, which originates with the ancient Romans, is the less well-known Ladin influence. The Ladin people are a minority tribe inhabiting various Dolomite valleys with their language and traditions. Their food comprises straightforward, unfussy recipes frequently produced with crops that may thrive in the complex alpine environment, such as corn, potatoes, barley, beans, etc.

The Standard Dishes

There are a variety of foods that are distinctive to the Dolomites, but a few of the most well-known ones are:

Tris di Canederli: This recipe calls for three sizable bread balls cooked in butter or broth with speck (smoked ham), cheese, or spinach. It was created as a method to use up leftover bread and is a filling and comforting dish.

Casunziei: These raviolis are fashioned like a half-moon and filled with beetroot or pumpkin. They are then topped with poppy seeds and melted butter. They are a delicacy that highlights the originality and vibrancy of regional cooking.

Polenta is a traditional food from cornmeal that is boiled in milk or water and served with cheese, pork, mushrooms, or vegetables. It is frequently referred to as "the bread of the Dolomites" since it serves as the primary source of carbohydrates for the inhabitants of the mountains.

Game meat is obtained by hunting and preparing a variety of wild species found in the Dolomites, including deer, roe deer, chamois, and ibex. Ibex roast, chamois stew, and venison with blueberries are some of the most popular meals.

Thin pastry layers packed with apples, raisins, cinnamon, and almonds make the dessert apfelstrudel. It is a prime illustration of how German culture has influenced regional sweets.

The Standard Drinks

The Dolomites also provide a variety of beverages to go with their meals or to enjoy on their own. Here are a few of the most prevalent:

Wine: The Dolomites are renowned for producing top-notch red, white, and sparkling wines, including Teroldego, Marzemino, Pinot Grigio, and Gewürztraminer. These wines go well with cheese, meat, and pasta dishes since they are fruity, fragrant, and well-balanced.

Brewing beer is a long-standing tradition in the Dolomites, particularly in the South Tyrol region. Regional breweries create beer varieties, including lager, pilsner, weissbier, and bock. Beers that pair well with bread, sausages, and dumplings are crisp, malty, and hopped.

Schnapps: This potent alcoholic beverage is created by distilling fruits or herbs. Apple, pear, cherry, or juniper berries are frequently used to flavour them. Typically, it is offered as a digestif following a meal or as a hot beverage in the winter.

Grappa is another potent alcoholic beverage manufactured from distilled grape pomace, which is left over after creating wine. It is clear or aged in wooden barrels and tastes sharp and robust. It is often used as a digestif or a cold cure.

CHAPTER 6

DOLOMITE OUTDOOR RECREATION

A stunning mountain range in northern Italy, the Dolomites have been recognized by UNESCO as a World Heritage Site because of their aesthetic value and cultural significance. For those who prefer being outside, they are a well-liked vacation spot where they may participate in a variety of activities in various climates and environments. The top outdoor activities in the Dolomites and the reasons you should attempt them are discussed in this essay.

Cycling

The most well-liked and gratifying method of discovering the Dolomites is by bicycle. Numerous roads, trails, and routes in the area cover hundreds of kilometres and accommodate all tastes and skill levels. You can ride a bicycle through quaint towns, gorgeous lakes, lovely valleys, and high passes. Giro d'Italia's legendarily tricky routes, like the Sella Ronda, Passo Pordoi, and Passo Giau, are also available to test your limits. An excellent way to get in shape, take in the scenery, and learn about the culture and history of the region is to go cycling in the Dolomites.

Hiking

The Dolomites can also be enjoyed via hiking. Numerous walking pathways, from short strolls to strenuous treks, may be found throughout the area. Mountains, meadows, alpine pastures, and woodlands are all accessible via hiking. The Tre Cime di Lavaredo, the Cinque Torri, the Seceda, and the Alpe di Siusi may all be reached by foot, along with other well-known Dolomites attractions. Going into nature and taking in the sights, wildlife, and plants while hiking in the Dolomites is a beautiful experience. Another option is to go on a hut-to-hut hiking expedition, where you may spend the night in snug mountain huts and sample the cuisine and hospitality of the locals.

Rope Climbing

The Dolomites are a great place to rock climb and engage in other thrilling activities. Some of the best climbing routes in the world may be found on the region's vertical walls, spires, and towers. From simple sport climbs to challenging traditional climbs, you may choose routes to suit your level of expertise. A protected climbing route that uses metal cables, ladders, and bridges is called via Ferrata, and you can also try one of those. It's exhilarating to test your physical and mental prowess when rock climbing in the Dolomites, where you can also take in the beauty from a new angle.

Skiing

In the Dolomites, during the winter, skiing is one of the most popular pastimes. Over 1200 kilometres of slopes in the area offer a variety of levels of difficulty and preferences, making it home to some of Europe's top ski resorts. Skiers can choose cross-country tracks, groomed slopes, or off-piste terrain. The Sellaronda, Marmolada, and Val Gardena are just a few of the world's most renowned ski runs you can use for skiing. Skiing in the Dolomites is an excellent opportunity to enjoy the winter paradise that this area transforms into, in addition to being a fun and thrilling pastime.

climbing in the Alps

Other challenging wintertime activities in the Dolomites include alpine mountaineering. Some of the world's most stunning peaks and ridges can be found in this area, which also boasts some of the best alpine routes on the planet. Crampons, ice axes, and ropes can be used to climb on ice, snow, or mixed terrain. Additionally, you can attempt some of the renowned mountaineers Reinhold Messner, Emilio Comici, and Walter Bonatti's legendary ascents. In the

Dolomites, alpine mountaineering is a daring method to test your limits and take in the roughness and beauty of the surroundings.

The Dolomites' Parks and Gardens

A stunning mountain range in northern Italy, UNESCO has designated the Dolomites as a World Heritage Site. for their natural beauty and cultural significance. They are a haven for those who enjoy the outdoors, where they may marvel at the region's diverse and abundant flora and animals. Visits to the parks and gardens that preserve and highlight the Dolomites' natural splendor are among the best ways to take in their beauty. In this paper, I will discuss some of the Dolomites' most stunning and fascinating parks and gardens and why you should see them.

Parks, both national and natural

Numerous national and natural parks may be found in the Dolomites, which occupy a sizable portion of the mountain range and protect its ecosystems, sceneries, and species. These parks provide a range of possibilities for tourists to learn about the Dolomites' natural history, including hiking paths, opportunities to observe wildlife, educational games, museums, and visitor centers. In the Dolomites, a few of the most significant parks are:

The province of Belluno is home to the 32,000-hectare Dolomiti Bellunesi National Park. It is distinguished by its untamed and rocky landscape, which includes high cliffs, narrow valleys, waterfalls, and caves. With more than 1,500 plant species and 124 bird species, it has a diverse range of flora and fauna. Additionally, it protects human historical artifacts like fortifications, cathedrals, and ancient communities.

The municipality of Cortina d'Ampezzo is home to the 11,200-hectare Dolomiti d'Ampezzo Natural Park. With its 1990 founding, it is one of Italy's oldest parks. It includes some of the Dolomites' most recognizable peaks, including the Tofane, the Cristallo, and the Croda Rossa. With more than 1,200 plant types and 203 bird species, it has a broad range of flora and animals. Additionally, it has cultural attractions such as monuments, museums, and archaeological sites.

Dolomiti Friulane Natural Park: Located in the provinces of Pordenone and Udine, this park spans 36,950 hectares. It is one of the Dolomites' most pristine and unspoiled regions, with little evidence of human intervention. It has stunning rock formations like the Spalti di Toro and the Campanile di

Val Montana. With more than 1,800 plant species and 149 bird species, it is also home to a diverse range of flora and animals.

Additionally, it protects cultural heritage, including folklore, traditional crafts, and villages.

The province of Bolzano is home to the 25,680-hectare Fanes-Senes-Braies Natural Park. One of the Dolomites' most gorgeous and varied regions, it features breathtaking vistas, including the Fanes Plateau, Sennes Alp, and Braies Lake. With over 2,000 plant and 203 bird species, it is also home to a diverse range of flora and animals. The language, customs, and tales of the Ladin people are also preserved.

The province of Bolzano is home to the 10,722-hectare Puez-Odle Natural Park. With all the rock varieties typical of this mountain range, it is one of the most representative regions of the Dolomites. It has breathtaking scenery, including the Seceda Ridge, Odle group, and Puez plateau. With more than 1,300 plant species and 162 bird species, it is also home to a diverse range of flora and fauna. Additionally, it protects cultural heritage, including old farms, churches, and traditions.

The province of Bolzano is home to the 7,291-hectare Sciliar-Catinaccio Natural Park. With its distinctive peaks, the

Sciliar massif and the Catinaccio group, it is one of the most iconic areas of the Dolomites. It has a variety of landscapes, including forests and meadows.

Tre Cime Natural Park: Located in the provinces of Bolzano and Belluno, this park spans 11,891 hectares. Its recognizable landmark, the Tre Cime di Lavaredo, is one of the Dolomites' most well-known and frequently visited regions. It has stunning natural scenery, including cliffs, pinnacles, and lakes. With more than 1,500 plant species and 135 bird species, it is also home to a diverse range of flora and fauna. It also maintains historical heritage, such as fortifications, trenches, and memorials from the First World War.

Natural Park of Paneveggio-Pale di San Martino: This park spans 19,717 hectares in Trento. With its contrasting landscapes—the Paneveggio forest, the Pale di San Martino plateau, and the Lagorai chain—it is one of the Dolomites' most exciting and diverse regions. With more than 1,600 plant species and 124 bird species, it is also home to a diverse range of flora and fauna. It also preserves cultural assets, such as musical instruments, art, and architecture.

Adamello-Brenta Natural Park: This park encompasses an area of 62,051 hectares in the province of Trento. It is the largest protected area in Trentino and one of the most important in the Alps. It contains two mountain groups: the Adamello-Presanella and the Brenta Dolomites. It has different scenery, such as glaciers, waterfalls, and canyons. It also has diverse flora and fauna, with over 1,800 plant species and 124 bird species. It also preserves cultural treasures, such as castles, museums, and traditions.

Its Gardens

The Dolomites are home to natural parks and gardens that exhibit the beauty and richness of the plants of this region. These gardens are places to enjoy flowers and trees and learn about their qualities, uses, and protection. Some of the most beautiful and intriguing gardens in the Dolomites are:

The Botanical Garden of Cortina d'Ampezzo: **This garden is positioned at a height of 1,700 meters.**

in Cortina d'Ampezzo. It was formed in 1974 by a group of local botanists who sought to preserve and study the alpine flora of the Dolomites. The garden covers an area of 2 hectares and supports approximately 500 plant species from different environments and altitudes. The garden also offers educational events, guided tours, and exhibitions.

The Alpine Garden Rezia is a garden in Bormio situated at a height of 1,560 meters. It was established in 1985 by local enthusiasts who desired to establish a living museum of the

Stelvio National Park's alpine flora. More than 2,000 plant species from various countries and continents are included in the garden, with a surface area of 1 hectare. The garden also hosts events, tours, and educational programs.

The Botanical Garden Alpino Viote is situated on Monte Bondone at a height of 1,550 meters. It was established in 1938 by local academics who wished to promote and safeguard Trentino's alpine flora. Over 2,000 plant species from various mountain ranges and climates are present in the 10-hectare garden. The garden also provides workshops, tours, and educational opportunities.

Dolomite Walking and Cycling Tours

They are an excellent place for those who enjoy walking and bicycling because they may go on several excursions in various climes. In this article, I'll go through some of the best biking and walking trips in the Dolomites and explain why you should try them.

Pedestrian Tours

One of the best ways to experience the Dolomites is via walking. There are various walking trails across the area, from strolls to strenuous expeditions. You can traverse rocky ground, meadows, alpine pastures, and woodlands while walking. You can also stroll to some of the Dolomites' most well-known sights, like the Seceda, the Cinque Torri, the Tre Cime di Lavaredo, and the Alpe di Siusi. Walking in the Dolomites is a fantastic way to get close to nature and enjoy the scenery, fauna, and plants.

A hut-to-hut walking tour is another option, where you can spend the night in snug mountain huts and sample the locals' cuisine.

In the Dolomites, a few of the top walking trips are:

Among the most popular and stunning long-distance trails in the Alps is the Alta Via 1. It travels 120 kilometers from Lake Braies to Belluno, passing through some of the most picturesque parts of the Dolomites, including the Civetta massif, the Pelmo group, the Lagazuoi-Cinque Torri region, and the Fanes-Sennes-Braies Natural Park. The whole thing takes roughly ten days to accomplish, with six hours of walking each day on average.

Lake Garda to the Brenta Dolomites: **This traditional hike marries Lake Garda's Mediterranean appeal with the untamed splendor of the Brenta Dolomites. It begins in the well-known ski resort of Madonna di Campiglio and ends in the charming lakeside town of Riva del Garda. Eighty kilometers are covered over six days, averaging 5 hours of walking each day.**

With all the rock types typical of this mountain range, the Puez-Odle Natural Park is one of the most representative locations of the Dolomites. It has a breathtaking landscape, including the Seceda Ridge, Odle group, and Puez plateau. The walking possibilities range from half-day strolls to all-day hikes, with varying degrees of difficulty.

bicycle tours

Exploring the Dolomites on a bike is yet another fantastic option. The area includes hundreds of kilometers of roads, trails, and paths to accommodate every desire and level of difficulty. You may ride through quaint towns, gorgeous lakes, picturesque valleys, and up to high passes. The Sella Ronda, the Passo Pordoi, and the Passo Giau are a few of the iconic roads that have been a part of the Giro d'Italia that you can test yourself on. Cycling in the Dolomites is a fantastic opportunity to get in shape, take in the scenery, and learn about the local history and culture.

In the Dolomites, some of the top biking excursions include:

One of the most renowned and well-liked bicycle circuits in the Alps is called the Sella Ronda. It travels in a circle around the Sella massif while traversing the Campolongo, Pordoi, Sella, and Gardena passes. It travels for roughly 55 kilometers and gains 1,800 meters in altitude.

Starting from any of the following points, it can be completed either clockwise or counterclockwise

The Tour of Marmolada is a strenuous bicycle ride that leads to the base of the Marmolada, the highest peak in the Dolomites. It begins in Alleghe, a lovely village on the same-named lake, and ends at Arabba, a well-known ski resort. It travels for around 70 kilometers and gains 2,300 meters in altitude. It travels over the Fedaia, Pordoi, and Campolongo passes.

The Dolomites Adventure is an action-packed bike tour that visits some of the most exciting and diverse regions of the Dolomites, including the Fanes-Sennes-Braies Natural Park, the Tre Cime di Lavaredo, the Cortina d'Ampezzo Valley, and the Val Gardena. With an average daily distance of 50 kilometers, it travels approximately 250 kilometers in 5 days. It incorporates off-road segments and combines road and mountain biking.

The Dolomites during the winter

They are a well-liked vacation spot for those who love the winter because they offer a variety of activities in various climates and surroundings. In this piece, I'll discuss some of the top winter sports you may enjoy in the Dolomites and why you should give them a shot.

Skiing

In the Dolomites, skiing is among the most well-liked and thrilling wintertime pastimes. With more than 1,200 kilometers of slopes that accommodate every ability level and preference, the area is home to some of the top ski resorts in Europe. Skiing is possible on cross-country paths, off-piste terrain, and groomed slopes. Some of the most well-known ski runs in the world, including the Sella Ronda, Marmolada, and Val Gardena, are also accessible. Skiing in the Dolomites is a thrilling and entertaining pastime allowing you to enjoy the area's winter magnificence.

Snowshoeing

Another fantastic winter activity in the Dolomites is snowshoeing. Numerous snowshoeing trails may be found in the area, ranging from straightforward strolls to strenuous hikes. You may snowshoe through forests, meadows, alpine pastures, and rocky terrain. You may also go snowshoeing to some of the Dolomites' most stunning and quiet areas, such as the Cinque Torri, the Fanes-Sennes-Braies Natural Park, and the Tre Cime di Lavaredo. Going snowshoeing in the Dolomites is a great way to get close to nature and take in the scenery, wildlife, and plants.

Paragliding

Another exhilarating activity you may enjoy in the Dolomites during the winter is paragliding. With breathtaking vistas of the craggy peaks, valleys, and lakes, the area has some of the best paragliding spots in the Alps. With qualified instructors and guides, you can fly solo or tandem. Additionally, you have various flight options, including cross-country, acrobatic, and panoramic flights. In the Dolomites, paragliding is an exhilarating opportunity to push your limits and take in the scenery from a new angle.

Sledding

Another enjoyable and simple winter sport in the Dolomites is sledding. The area has numerous sledding hills, with options for every skill level and taste. Sledding is possible on natural and artificial tracks, with or without lifts. The Alpe di Siusi track, which is 6 kilometers long, and the San Candido track, which is 5 kilometers long, are two of the longest and most beautiful sledding routes in the Alps.

A fun activity to enjoy the snow and speed with your loved ones is sledding in the Dolomites.

Nordic Walking and Trekking

Another wholesome and calming activity you may engage in during the winter in the Dolomites is trekking or Nordic walking. Numerous Nordic walking and hiking trails may be found in the area, ranging from straightforward strolls to strenuous hikes. You can traverse rocky ground, meadows, alpine pastures, and woodlands while walking. Some of the most famous Dolomites monuments, like the Sciliar massif, the Catinaccio group, and the Lagazuoi-Cinque Torri region, are also accessible on foot. In the Dolomites, trekking or Nordic walking is a fantastic way to exercise and get fresh air.

CHAPTER 7

LOCATIONS NEAR THE DOLOMITES

The magnificent Dolomites mountain range is in northeastern Italy and is part of the northern Italian Alps. They cover seven provinces (South Tyrol, Trentino, Verona, Vicenza, Belluno, Udine, and Pordenone) and three Italian regions (Veneto, Trentino-Alto Adige/Südtirol, and Friuli Venezia Giulia). The valleys of the Isarco, Pusteria, Piave, Brenta, and Adige surround them.

The peak reaches over 11,000 feet above sea level at its highest point. The Dolomites are well-known for their scenic beauty, cultural richness, and recreational opportunities. What about the Dolomites' surroundings, though? Beyond the magnificent peaks and valleys, what more is there to see and do? I'll discuss some of the Dolomites' most fascinating and alluring surroundings and explain why traveling there is worthwhile.

Bolzano

The capital of South Tyrol is Bolzano, which is also a primary entryway to the Dolomites. It is a lovely city blending German and Italian influences in its culture, cuisine, and architecture. You can go to the Gothic cathedral, the famous ice mummy Tzi's modern museum, the Renaissance palace of

Runkelstein, the medieval castle of Mareccio, and the Gothic cathedral. Additionally, you may browse the vibrant markets, stroll along the arcaded streets, and savor regional specialties like strudel, knödel, and speck (smoked ham).

Garda Lake

Italy's largest lake, Lake Garda, is also one of the most visited places in the world. The turquoise lake and the green hills contrast this area, which is on the southern edge of the Dolomites. You can engage in sports on and around the lake, like sailing, windsurfing, kayaking, hiking, riding, and climbing. You can also stop at charming hamlets and towns that line the lakeshore, like Sirmione, Malcesine, Limone sul Garda, and Riva del Garda.

Venice

One of the world's most well-known and stunning cities, Venice is also a UNESCO World Heritage Site. It can be reached by vehicle or train in about two hours and is worth a day trip or an overnight stay from the Dolomites. The St. Mark's Basilica, the Doge's Palace, the Rialto Bridge, and the Grand Canal are just a few examples of Venice's distinctive architecture and artwork that you can admire. You may also tour the winding streets, secret plazas, and beautiful waterways by foot or gondola. Additionally, you can savor some of Italy's top cuisine and beverages, like prosecco, risotto, and other rice dishes.

Verona

Another lovely city in northern Italy is Verona, a UNESCO World Heritage Site. It is a fantastic location for cultural enthusiasts, around an hour's drive or train ride from the Dolomites. Verona's historical and artistic highlights include the Roman Arena, where opera performances are presented during the summer, the medieval Castelvecchio Castle, the Romanesque Cathedral, and Juliet's House, where you can see the fabled balcony from Shakespeare's play. You can also savor regional specialties like Amarone (red wine), polenta, and gnocchi (potato dumplings).

CHAPTER 8

ITINERARY FOR 7 DAYS IN THE DOLOMITES

The magnificent Dolomites mountain range is in northeastern Italy and is part of the northern Italian Alps. They cover seven provinces (South Tyrol, Trentino, Verona, Vicenza, Belluno, Udine, and Pordenone) and three Italian regions (Veneto, Trentino-Alto Adige/Südtirol, and Friuli Venezia Giulia). The valleys of the Isarco, Pusteria, Piave, Brenta, and Adige surround them.

The peak reaches over 11,000 feet above sea level at its highest point. The Dolomites are well-known for their scenic beauty, cultural richness, and recreational opportunities. They provide a range of chances for tourists to learn about the region's vegetation, animals, history, and culture. How to maximize your time and experience the best of the Dolomites may be on your mind if you intend to travel there.

I have put together a 7-day itinerary that includes some of the highlights of the Dolomites to assist you with that. This route is based on a car drive, but if you'd rather, you may also take public transportation or sign up for a tour. This schedule can also be altered to suit your preferences and interests. How to spend a week in the Dolomites is as follows:

Day 1 Bolzano and Lake Carezza

Bolzano, the capital of South Tyrol and one of the primary entryways to the Dolomites, is an excellent place to start your journey. In Bolzano's architecture, culture, and food, Italian and German influences can be found. You can go to the Gothic cathedral, the famous ice mummy Tzi's modern museum, the Renaissance palace of Runkelstein, the medieval castle of Mareccio, and the Gothic cathedral.

Additionally, you may browse the vibrant markets, stroll along the arcaded streets, and savor regional specialties like strudel, knödel, and speck (smoked ham). In the afternoon, drive to Lake Carezza, one of the Dolomites' most stunning lakes. The spikey peaks of the Latemar mountain range are reflected in Lake Carezza, a sparkling turquoise body of water.

You can take a boat ride or a stroll around the lake to soak in its splendor. Visit the Grand Hotel Carezza, where notable visitors like Winston Churchill and Agatha Christie formerly lodged, or the Carezza ski resort, where you can engage in winter activities if you go there in the winter.

Day 2 Sella Ronda and Cortina d'Ampezzo

Drive to Canazei, a charming village in Val di Fassa, where the Sella Ronda, one of the most well-known and picturesque circuits in the Alps, begins on your second day. The Sella Ronda is a circular path traversing via the Campolongo, Pordoi, Sella, and Gardena as it travels around the Sella massif.

It travels for roughly 55 kilometers and gains 1,800 meters in altitude. Starting from any of the four passes, it can be done clockwise or counterclockwise. The Sella Ronda provides breathtaking views of some of the Dolomites' most recognizable peaks, including Marmolada, Sassolungo, and Tofane.

You can do it in the summer by vehicle or bicycle, while in the winter, you can ski or snowboard. You can stop at quaint towns along the journey, including Corvara, Arabba, and Selva di Val Gardena. The Pordoi cable car, which takes you to Sass Pordoi at 2,950 meters, and the Museum Ladin Ciastel de Tor, which presents the culture and history of the Ladin people that inhabit this region, are just a few of the attractions that are located along or close to the route.

After finishing the Sella Ronda, drive to Cortina d'Ampezzo, one of Italy's most renowned and opulent ski resorts. Cortina d'Ampezzo is a fashionable town with a wide selection of stores, eateries, and bars, as well as some cultural attractions like the Regole d'Ampezzo Ethnographic Museum, which showcases local crafts and costumes, or the Mario Rimoldi Modern Art Museum, which features some pieces by Italian artists like De Chirico, Morandi, and De Pisis.

Day 3: Lake Misurina and the Tre Cime di Lavaredo

On your third day, drive to Auronzo di Cadore, a little town at the base of the Tre Cime di Lavaredo, one of the most well-known and stunning sights in the Dolomites. The Tre Cime di Lavaredo is a trio of high peaks that reach more than 3,000 meters and stand out sharply from the surroundings. From several vantage points, such as the Rifugio Auronzo, the Rifugio Lavaredo, or the Rifugio Locatelli, you can observe them. You can also take a circular trail that travels around 10 kilometers and takes about 4 hours to hike around them. The hike offers breathtaking views of the mountains and valleys, as well as visits to some important historical monuments such as the Galleria del Paterno, a tunnel used by the Italian forces in World War I, or the Cappella degli Alpini, a church honoring the war's lost warriors from that conflict. Drive to Lake Misurina, another lovely Dolomite lake, after hiking the Tre Cime di Lavaredo. A tranquil lake, Lake Misurina mirrors the Sorapiss, Cristallo, and Cadini di Misurina peaks. To experience the peace of the lake, go for a walk around it or rent a boat. You may also check out some neighboring sights, including the Tre Cime Natural Park, a protected area with diverse plants and animals, or the Cadini di Misurina, a collection of rocky pinnacles that provide challenging climbing routes.

Day 4: Val Gardena and Alpe di Siusi

On the fourth day, drive to Alpe di Siusi, Europe's most prominent and highest alpine meadow. At a height of 1,800 to 2,300 meters, Alpe di Siusi has a surface area of 56 square kilometers. It provides a breathtaking view of several of the most magnificent Dolomites peaks, including Sassolungo, Sciliar, and Catinaccio. You can use the many trails and paths in Alpe di Siusi to go hiking, biking, or riding a horse. If you go in the winter, you can also engage in winter sports like skiing, snowshoeing, or sledding. You can pause at quaint mountain huts along the road providing food and beverages, including the Rifugio Molignon, the Rifugio Alpe di Tires, or the Rifugio Zallinger. You can also go to some of the sights that are on or close to Alpe di Siusi, including the Castelrotto Golf Club, an 18-hole course that provides a distinctive golfing experience in the Dolomites, or the Sciliar-Catinaccio Natural Park.

This protected region is home to a diverse flora and fauna. Drive to Val Gardena, one of the most stunning and well-known valleys in the Dolomites, after touring Alpe di Siusi.

Three significant communities may be found in the 25-kilometer-long Val Gardena Valley: Ortisei, Santa Cristina, and Selva di Val Gardena. Val Gardena is renowned for its history of wood carving, the Ladin culture, and the Dolomiti Superski region's ski resorts.

You can check out some of Val Gardena's cultural and artistic attractions, such as the Gherdeina Museum, which showcases some woodcarving, paintings, and sculpture specimens, or the Church of San Giacomo, which has some frescoes by renowned painter Chierici.

You can also take advantage of some of the outdoor activities that Val Gardena provides, such as skiing, snowboarding, or ice skating on its slopes and rinks, hiking, riding, or climbing on its many trails and routes.

Day 5: Funes Valley and Lake Braies

On your fifth day, drive to Lake Braies, one of the Dolomites' most famous lakes, for Instagram photos. Beautiful Lake Braies has varying hues depending on the time of year and the light. The colors range from dark blue to turquoise blue to emerald green.

It is encircled by magnificent mountains like Croda del Becco and Monte Nero, as well as thick forests. Walking the 4 kilometers around the lake takes roughly an hour on a simple track. You can also take a boat trip to appreciate the lake's beauty from a new angle. You may also check out some of the adjacent sights, including the Braies Wild Lake, a smaller lake that is less crowded and is located at an elevation of 2,000 meters, or the Prato Piazza.

This high plateau provides panoramic views of the Dolomites. Drive to Funes Valley, one of the most beautiful valleys in the Dolomites, after visiting Lake Braies. Funes Valley is a valley that is 1,000 to 2,500 meters above sea level and is home to Santa Maddalena, San Pietro, and San Valentino, among other communities.

The picturesque panorama of green meadows, wooden chalets, and churches with onion-shaped domes makes Funes Valley famous.

Also famous is its picture-perfect view of the Geisler peaks, which is frequently shown on calendars and postcards. Funes Valley's numerous trails and paths can be used for hiking, biking, or horseback riding exploration. If you go in the winter, you can also engage in winter sports like skiing, snowshoeing, or sledding.

You can pause at quaint mountain huts along the road providing food and beverages, including the Rifugio Genova, the Rifugio Firenze, or the Rifugio Puez. You can also check out some of the sights in or close to Funes Valley, such as the Puez-Odle Natural Park, a preserve with a diverse array of plants and animals, or the Adolf Munkel Trail, a scenic route that follows the foot of the Geisler peaks.

Day 6: Passo Giau and Marmolada

Drive to Marmolada on your sixth day, the highest peak in the Dolomites and one of the most stunning and rugged summits in the Alps. The southern face of Marmolada, which rises to a height of 3,342 meters, is covered in a glacier.

From several vantage points, such as the Passo Fedaia, the Passo Pordoi, or the Passo San Pellegrino, you may admire

Marmolada. You can also take a cable car to Punta Rocca, which is located at a height of 3,265 meters, from where you can see the Dolomites in all their beauty and visit the Museum of the Great War, which features relics and records from World War I. On Marmolada, you can hike or climb, but only if you are a skilled climber with the proper gear. The Via Ferrata degli Alleghesi, the Via Ferrata della Cresta Ovest, and the Via Ferrata Eterna are just a few of Marmolada's challenging and rewarding paths.

After appreciating Giau, one of the Dolomites' most picturesque and panoramic passes, drive to Passo Marmolada. The 2,236-meter-high Passo Giau connects Colle Santa Lucia with Cortina d'Ampezzo. It provides a beautiful view of several well-known Dolomites peaks, including Tofane, Croda da Lago, Nuvolau, and Averau—the numerous pathways and paths in Passo Giau suit biking or walking.

If you go in the winter, you can also engage in winter sports like skiing, snowshoeing, or sledding. You can pause at quaint mountain huts along the road providing food and beverages, including the Rifugio Averau, the Rifugio Fedare, or the Rifugio Passo Giau.

You can also check out some sights close to Passo Giau, such as the Cinque Torri, rock formations offering incredible climbing routes, or the Lagazuoi. This mountain is home to several World War I-era historical structures, including tunnels, galleries, and bunkers.

7th day: Departure

Drive back to Bolzano or Venice on your seventh and last day, depending on where you arrived. To extend your journey, visit any other Dolomite's neighboring regions, such as Lake Garda, Verona, or Trento. Additionally, you can travel to other parts of Italy, including Tuscany, Sicily, and Sardinia.

CHAPTER 9

PRACTICAL INFORMATION AND TIPS FOR DOLOMITES

Etiquette and Customs in Dolomites

A stunning mountain range in Italy called the Dolomites northeastern Italy lies in the eastern section of the northern Italian Alps. They span three regions of Italy (Veneto, Trentino-Alto Adige/Südtirol, and Friuli Venezia Giulia) and seven provinces (South Tyrol, Trentino, Verona, Vicenza, Belluno, Udine, and Pordenone). The valleys of the Isarco, the Pusteria, the Piave, the Brenta, and the Adige bound them. The highest point of the mountain rises nearly 11,000 feet above sea level.

The Dolomites are famous for their natural beauty, cultural diversity, and outdoor activities. They offer a variety of opportunities for visitors to discover the flora and fauna of this region, as well as its history and culture. If you visit the Dolomites, you might wonder how to behave and what to expect from the local people and culture.

To help you with that, I have compiled some etiquette and customs tips to make your trip more respectful and enjoyable. Here is what you need to know about etiquette and customs in the Dolomites:

Language and Greetings

The Dolomites are a multilingual area with four languages: Italian, German, Ladin, and Friulian. Italian is the nation's official and most widely spoken language in the Dolomites. German is spoken mainly in South Tyrol, where it is co-official with Italian. Ladin is a Romance language derived from Latin spoken by about 30,000 people in five valleys around the Sella group: Val Gardena, Val Badia, Val di Fassa, Livinallongo, and Ampezzo. Friulian is another Romance language derived from Latin spoken by about 600,000 people in Friuli Venezia Giulia, especially in Udine and Pordenone provinces. You may encounter different languages and dialects depending on where you are in the Dolomites. Learning some essential words and phrases in each language is advisable to communicate with the locals and show respect for their culture. You can find some valuable resources here:

Italian phrases

German phrases

Ladin phrases

Friulian phrases

When greeting someone in the Dolomites, you can use different forms of salutation depending on the language and the situation. Here are some common ways to say hello and goodbye:

In Italian: Buongiorno (good morning/day), Buonasera (good evening), Ciao (hello/goodbye), Arrivederci (goodbye), Salve (hello)

In German: Guten Morgen (good morning), Guten Tag (good day), Guten Abend (good evening), Hallo (hello), Tschüss (goodbye), Auf Wiedersehen (goodbye)

In Ladin: Bongiorn (good morning/day), Bona sera (good evening), Salüd (hello/goodbye), A revëider (goodbye)

In Friulian: Bondì (good morning/day), Bon sera (good evening), Mandi (hello/goodbye), A ravioli (goodbye)

When meeting someone for the first time or in a formal setting, it is polite to shake hands and use titles such as Signore/Signora (Mr./Mrs.) in Italian or Herr/Frau (Mr./Mrs.) in German. You can also use Lei/Sie (you) to address someone in Italian or German formally. When meeting someone you know or in a casual setting, you can kiss on both cheeks or hug as a sign of affection. You can also use tu/du (you) as an informal way of addressing someone in Italian or German.

Dress Code and Behavior

The Dolomites are a relaxed and friendly area where people dress casually and comfortably according to the season and the occasion. However, there are some general rules of etiquette and behavior that you should follow to avoid offending or disrespecting anyone. Here are some tips:

For the weather and the activities, wear proper clothing.

Wear warm clothes such as jackets, sweaters, hats, gloves, and boots in winter. Wear light garments such as shirts, shorts, dresses, and sandals in summer. However, avoid wearing revealing or skimpy clothes, especially in religious or conservative places. Dress modestly and respectfully, especially when visiting churches, museums, or monuments.

Dress smartly for formal or special occasions. If you are invited to a wedding, a dinner, or a concert, wear elegant clothes such as suits, dresses, ties, and shoes. Avoid wearing jeans, sneakers, t-shirts, or hats. In general, dress according to the event's dress code or the place.

Respect the environment and nature. A UNESCO World Heritage Site, the Dolomites protected area with rich flora and fauna. When visiting the Dolomites, be mindful of your impact on the environment and nature. Do not litter, do not pick flowers or plants, do not feed or disturb animals, do not make noise or fire, and do not camp or park illegally. Generally, follow the rules and regulations of the gardens and the trails.

Respect the culture and the tradition. The Dolomites are a diverse and multicultural area where different languages, customs, and traditions coexist. When visiting the Dolomites, be curious and open-minded about the local people's culture and traditions. Learn some words and phrases in their languages, try some of their dishes and specialties, participate in festivals and events, and listen to some of their stories and legends. In general, they show interest and appreciation for their culture and tradition.

Knowing Some Basic Dolomite Phrases

Dolomites are also home to three different languages? Italian, German, and Ladin are all spoken in other parts of the region, reflecting its rich and diverse history and culture. If you plan to visit the Dolomites, learn some simple phrases in each language to communicate with the locals and appreciate their traditions.

Here are some of the most common and helpful expressions to know in the Dolomites:

Italian

Italy's official language is Italian, and

the most widely spoken in the Dolomites. Some areas, such as Cortina d'Ampezzo, are predominantly Italian in culture and language. Latin gave rise to the Romance language of Italian.

Which shares similarities with other languages like Spanish, French, and Portuguese. Here are some basic Italian phrases to get you started:

Hello: Ciao (informal) or Salve (formal)

Good morning / good day: Buon giorno

Good evening: Buona sera

Good night: Buona notte

Good bye: Arrivederci

Please: Per piacere or per favore

Thank you: Grazie

Thank you very much: Grazie mille

You're welcome: Prego

Do you speak English? (formal): Parla inglese?

Do you speak English? (informal): Parli inglese?

I don't speak Italian: Non parlo Italiano

I don't understand: Non-capisco

Excuse me / sorry: Mi scusi or scusa

How are you? (formal): Come sta?

How are you? (informal): Come stai?

I'm fine, thank you: Sto bene, Grazie

What is your name? (formal): Come si chiama?

What is your name? (informal): Come ti chiami?

My name is...: Mi chiamo...

Nice to meet you: Piacere di conoscerti or piacere di conoscerla

Where are you from? (formal): Di dove è?

Where are you from? (informal): Di dove sei?

I'm from...: Sono di...

How much is it? Quanto costa?

Where is...? Dov'è...?

Can I have...? Posso avere...?

The bill, please: Il conto, per favor

Cheers! Salute or cin cin

German

German is the primary language spoken in the northern part of the Dolomites, also known as Südtirol (in German) or Alto Adige (in Italian). This area was part of the Austro-Hungarian empire until the end of World War I, when Italy annexed it. However, most of the population still identifies as German-speaking and maintains a strong cultural connection with Austria. German is a Germanic language related to English, Dutch, and Scandinavian languages. Here are some essential German phrases to get you started:

Hello: Hallo

Good morning / good day: Guten Morgen / Guten Tag

Good evening: Guten Abend

Good night: Gute Nacht

Good bye: Aufwiedersehen

Please: Bitte

Thank you: Danke

Thank you very much: Vielen Dank or Dankeschön

You're welcome: Bitte or Bitteschön

Do you speak English? Sprechen Sie Englisch?

I don't speak German: Ich spreche kein Deutsch

I don't understand: Ich verstehe nicht

Excuse me / sorry: Entschuldigung or es tut mir leid

How are you? Wie geht es Ihnen? (formal) or Wie geht's? (informal)

I'm fine, thank you: Mir geht es gut, danke

What is your name? Wie heißen Sie? (formal) or Wie heißt du? (informal)

My name is... Ich heiße...

Nice to meet you: Freut mich, Sie kennenzulernen (formal) or Freut mich, dich kennenzulernen (informal)

Where are you from? Woher kommen Sie? (formal) or Woher kommst du? (informal)

I'm from... Ich komme aus...

How much is it? Wie viel kostet das?

Where is...? Wo ist...?

Can I have...? Kann ich...haben?

The bill, please: Die Rechnung, bitte

Cheers! Prost

Ladin

Ladin is an ancient Romance language spoken by about 30,000 people in the Dolomites, mainly in the five Ladin valleys: Val Gardena, Alta Badia, Cortina d'Ampezzo, Fodom, and Val di Fassa. The oldest language in the area is Ladin, which was influenced by the Latin-speaking Romans who settled there. Ladin has several dialects and variations, but a standard form called Dolomite Ladin has been developed as a common communication tool across the Ladin-speaking areas. Ladin is recognized as a minority language and has some official status in South Tyrol, Trentino, and Belluno provinces. Here are some basic Ladin phrases to get you started:

Hello: Ciao (informal) or Bun dé (formal)

Good morning / good day: Bun dé

Good evening: Buna sëra

Good night: Buna nöt

Goodbye: Assudëi

Please: Prëitambel

Thank you: Giulan

Thank you very much: Dër bel giulan

You're welcome: Nia da dì

Do you speak English? (formal): La parla ingles?

Do you speak English? (informal): Te parles ingles?

I don't speak Ladin: No parlo ladin'

I don't understand: No capìs

Excuse me / sorry: Scusé or Scusa

How are you? (formal): Co va la?

How are you? (informal): Co vas te?

I'm fine, thank you: Va bën, giulan

What is your name? (formal): Co se clama la?

What is your name? (informal): Co te clames te?

My name is... Me clamor...

Nice to meet you: Piacë de cognoscerla (formal) or Piacë de cognoscerte (informal)

Where are you from? (formal): De do la é?

Where are you from? (informal): De do te es te?

I'm from... So de...

How much is it? Cianto costa?

Where is...? Ando é...?

Can I have...? Pòdo vëgnir...?

The bill, please: La nota, prëitambel

Cheers! Salùt or cin cin

As you can see, the Dolomites are a fascinating linguistic and cultural mosaic that offers a unique experience to visitors. Learning some simple phrases in each language can help you interact with the locals and show respect for their heritage. You might also discover some interesting similarities and differences between the languages and learn more about their origins and evolution. So please don't be shy and give it a try! You might be surprised by how much fun it is to speak the languages of the Dolomites!

Health and safety tips in the Dolomites

The Dolomites are a breathtaking mountain range in northern Italy, renowned for their spectacular scenery, diverse culture, and outdoor activities. Whether you are hiking, biking, skiing, or climbing, the Dolomites offer endless opportunities for adventure and enjoyment. However, like any mountain environment, the Dolomites pose some risks and challenges requiring proper preparation and awareness. To ensure that you have a safe and healthy trip to the Dolomites, here are some tips to keep in mind:

1. Check the weather forecast and trail conditions

The weather in the Dolomites can change quickly and unpredictably, especially at higher altitudes. The weather forecast must be checked.

Before you head out for any activity and be prepared for different scenarios, you can find reliable weather information on websites such as www.meteotrentino.it or www.arpa.veneto.it. You should also check your chosen route's trail conditions and difficulty level and ensure it matches your skills and equipment. You can find updated trail information on websites such as www.sentres.com or www.dolomiti.org.

2. Dress appropriately and pack the essentials

The temperature in the Dolomites can vary significantly depending on the season, time of day, and elevation. Wear layers that are simple to take off.

You added or removed it according to the weather and your activity level. You should also wear appropriate footwear for good grip and support on rocky and uneven terrain. Some of the essential items to pack for any outdoor activity in the Dolomites are:

A waterproof jacket and pants

A warm fleece or sweater

A hat and gloves

A sun hat and sunglasses

Sunscreen and lip balm

A first-aid kit

A map and compass or GPS device

A flashlight or headlamp

A whistle

A water bottle and snacks

A trash bag

3. Stay hydrated and eat well

The Dolomites are located at high altitudes, meaning the air is thinner and drier than at sea level. This can cause dehydration, headaches, fatigue, and altitude sickness if you are not used to it. To prevent these problems, Throughout the day, make sure to stay hydrated and steer clear of coffee and alcohol.

You should also eat well-balanced meals that provide enough energy and nutrients for your activity level. You can find delicious local food in many restaurants, cafes, and rifugios (mountain huts) in the Dolomites or bring your food.

4. Follow the rules and respect the environment

A UNESCO World Heritage Site, the Dolomites

a protected natural area that hosts a rich biodiversity of flora and fauna. It will help if you respect the rules and regulations that aim to preserve this unique environment and its inhabitants. Some of the basic rules to follow are:

Stay on marked trails, and do not cut across switchbacks or meadows

Do not pick flowers or plants or disturb wildlife

Do not light fires or camp outside designated areas

Do not litter or leave any trace of your passage

Do not feed or approach wild animals

Do not make loud noises or play music

5. Be aware of potential hazards

The Dolomites are a beautiful but also a potentially dangerous place if you are not careful. Some of the hazards that you may encounter are:

Rockfalls and landslides can occur due to natural causes or human activity, especially after heavy rain or snowmelt. You should avoid walking under unstable cliffs or slopes and heed warning signs.

Avalanches can occur during winter or spring when snow accumulates on steep slopes. You should avoid crossing avalanche-prone areas and carry an avalanche transceiver, probe, and shovel if you are skiing or snowshoeing.

Thunderstorms: These can occur suddenly during summer or autumn, bringing strong winds, lightning, hail, and heavy rain. Avoid exposed ridges or summits during thunderstorms and seek shelter in a rifugio or a valley.

When your body temperature falls below average, you develop hypothermia.

Due to exposure to cold weather or water. You should wear warm clothing, stay dry, eat and drink regularly, and seek medical help if you experience symptoms such as shivering, confusion, drowsiness, or loss of coordination.

6. Know what to do in case of emergency

Despite your best efforts to prevent accidents or injuries, you may still encounter an emergency in the Dolomites. In this case, you should know how to get help immediately. Here are some steps to follow:

Assess the situation: Check if anyone is injured or in danger and try to stabilize their condition if possible. Only move them if they are in immediate danger or a rescuer instructs you.

Call for help: Use your phone or a nearby phone to call the emergency number 112. This universal number connects you to the local police, fire brigade, or mountain rescue service. Please give them your name, location, and details of the situation and follow their instructions.

Signal for help: If you cannot reach anyone by phone, you can use other methods to signal for help, such as a whistle, a flashlight, a mirror, or a brightly colored cloth. You can also use the international distress signal, three short blasts or flashes followed by a pause and repeated.

Stay calm and wait for help: Do not panic or lose hope. Keep yourself and others warm, hydrated, and comfortable until help arrives.

A List Of Dolomites Emergency Contacts

If you have an emergency in the Dolomites, such as an accident, injury, or illness, you should know how to call the relevant authorities and agencies for assistance. Italy and other European nations can call 112 in an emergency.

According to your needs, you can call this number to be connected to the neighborhood police, fire department, or mountain rescue service. Please give them your name, where you are located, and any other pertinent information on the emergency, then do what they say.

A whistle, a flashlight, a mirror, or a piece of clothing with a bold pattern can also signal aid. Another option is the international distress signal, consisting of three brief blasts or flashes followed by pausing and repeating.

There are a few other helpful people you might need in the Dolomites outside emergency number 112, including:

In the Dolomites, a volunteer group called Aiut Alpin Dolomites offers helicopter rescue services. You may reach them at +39 0471 786448 or +39 0471 797171 if you need more information or support. For additional advice on reporting an emergency and signaling for assistance, see their website at www.aiut-alpin-dolomites.com.

This service offers emergency medical attention to tourists and other visitors to the Dolomites. You can find their offices and phone lines in various places, such as Val Gardena, Alta Badia, Cortina d'Ampezzo, etc. To learn more, go to www.dolomitisuperski.com, which is also their website.

Local medical facilities and drug stores: You can go to a community hospital or pharmacy in the nearby town or village if you require medical care that is not urgent or life-threatening. Websites such as www.meteotrentino.it and www.arpa.veneto.it have their addresses and phone numbers.

You can have peace of mind while traveling to the Dolomites by knowing these emergency contacts and being safe and healthy there. By considering the safety advice provided above and being ready for anything, you should always aim to avoid mishaps or injuries.

Access to the Internet and communication in the Dolomites

When traveling to the Dolomites, communication, and internet availability are crucial factors, particularly if you need to access information or services online or want to stay in touch with your friends, family, or job. The alternatives and difficulties for communication and internet connectivity may vary depending on where you are in the Dolomites. The following advice will assist you:

1. Select a dependable phone plan and service.

Before visiting the Dolomites, foreign travelers should confirm their phone plan and provider. Find out whether your plan includes roaming fees in Italy and other European nations or whether you must purchase a local SIM card or a prepaid plan. In the Dolomites, you should also check your provider's coverage and signal quality because some places could have weak or no reception. Websites like www.prepaid-data-sim-card.fandom.com or www.whistleout.com include details on phone plans and carriers.

2. Make use of public internet access points or Wi-Fi hotspots

You can utilize Wi-Fi hotspots or public internet access points to connect to the Internet if you want to save money on data or phone calls or if there is no signal where you are. Many hotels, eateries, cafes, rifugios (mountain huts), tourist information centers, and other public locations in the Dolomites have Wi-Fi connections.

They might be accessible for customers or visitors, or you might have to sign up or pay a charge to use them. You can also find public internet connection points in some libraries, museums, or cultural institutions in the Dolomites. Websites like www.wificafespots.com or www.wififreespot.com have information on Wi-Fi hotspots and public internet access points.

3. Download content in advance or make use of offline apps.

You can utilize offline apps or download content in advance to use on your phone, tablet, or laptop if you want to avoid using data or Wi-Fi or if you have little to no internet connectivity in the Dolomites. You can utilize offline games, books, music, podcasts, films, dictionaries, guides, maps, and more. You can locate offline apps on websites like www.offline-apps.com or in-app shops like the Apple Store or Google Play.

Additionally, you can download material from websites like www.spotify.com, www.wikipedia.org, www.netflix.com, and www.google.com/maps.

4. Recognize any potential dangers and constraints.

In the Dolomites, access to the Internet and dependable communication are not always guaranteed. You should know of any dangers or restrictions limiting your ability to communicate or access the Internet while in the Dolomites. Among them are:

Weather: The speed and availability of phone and internet signals are impacted by the Dolomites' swift and unpredictable weather changes. Before leaving, you should check the weather prediction to be ready for various conditions.

Power outages: The Dolomites' power supply could be disrupted by human activity or natural disasters, impacting the functionality of phones and internet services. Your electronics should be charged frequently; you should bring a power bank or solar charger.

Cybersecurity: When using public Wi-Fi hotspots or internet access points, the Internet in the Dolomites may not be private or secure. Your devices and data should be secured against hackers, malware, viruses, phishing, and other threats. Use encryption software, strong passwords, a virtual private network (VPN), antivirus software, firewall software, etc.

Legal considerations: Especially regarding privacy, copyright, censorship, etc., the Internet in the Dolomites may be subject to different rules and regulations than in your home country. Respect your local laws and ordinances, and refrain from accessing or disseminating offensive or illegal online content.

Many visitors to the Dolomites depend on communication and internet connection. Using these suggestions, you can have a better relationship and internet access when traveling in the Dolomites and relax. Enjoy yourself, and keep in touch!

Useful apps and websites in the Dolomites:

The Dolomites are an excellent destination for travelers who love nature, culture, and adventure. However, planning a trip to the Dolomites can be difficult, especially if you need to learn more about

The region, its geography, its language, and its attractions. Fortunately, there are some useful apps and websites that can help you make the most of your trip to the Dolomites. Here are some of them:

1. Earth Trekkers

Earth Trekkers is a website that provides detailed guides and tips on planning a Dolomite trip. You can find information on the best time to visit, how to get around, where to stay, what to do, where to eat, and more. You can also find inspiration from their photos and videos of the Dolomites. Earth Trekkers is run by a family of four who have traveled extensively around the world and have visited the Dolomites several times. You can trust their advice and recommendations based on their personal experience. You can visit their website at www.earthtrekkers.com.

2. Hear Dolomites

Hear Dolomites is an app that offers audio guides about the Dolomites and the province of South Tyrol. You can learn more about this region's history, culture, traditions, and natural phenomena by listening to narrated stories and facts.

You can use this app by bus, car, or home. You can choose from different topics and languages and download the audio files for offline use. Hearing Dolomites is a great way to enrich your knowledge and appreciation of the Dolomites. This app is available on Google Play.

3. Dolomites Guide

Dolomites Guide is an app that helps you organize a one-week trip to the heart of the Dolomites starting from Cortina d'Ampezzo. This app provides a suggested itinerary covering the best places to see and things to do in the Dolomites. You can also find accommodation, transportation, weather, maps, and more information.

Using this app, you may save money and tailor your trip to your needs and financial constraints. The Dolomites Guide is a helpful resource for organizing an easy trip to the Dolomites. This app is available on Google Play.

You can arrange a journey to the Dolomites with these practical websites and applications. By employing these resources, you can save time, money, and effort while thoroughly enjoying your trip. Travel safely and enjoy yourself!

Conclusion

This guide is all you need to make your stay in this amazing country a memorable one. Wish you safe travels.

Made in the USA
Middletown, DE
22 May 2024